EFFECTIVE
REMOTE TEAMS

How To Lead Yourself And Your Team To Achieve Extraordinary Outcomes Without Burnout

Published by
BEVERLY HILLS PUBLISHING
468 Camden Drive

Beverly Hills, California 90210

Beverly Hills Publishing Inc.
www.beverlyhillspublishing.com

ISBN: 978-1-7378006-3-7

For every corporate leader who wants to lead their teams and themselves to work from wherever, whenever.

And for James, Angus, and Eliza—who give me reason to live and work in this way every day.

Table of Contents

PART 1
How to Lead Yourself

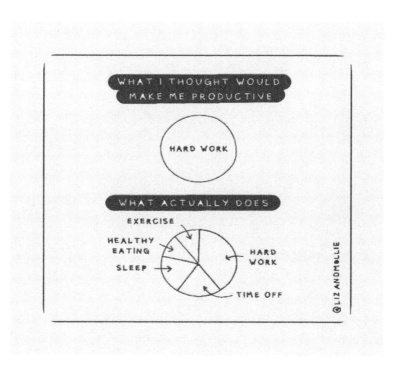

CHAPTER 1

Learn from My Biggest Mistake

"It's good to learn from your mistakes, but it's better to learn from some-one else's."
—Warren Buffet

It doesn't matter how smart you are, how strong you are, or how many decades of leadership you have, the new normal for corporate leaders is here. A paradigm shift has occurred right before our eyes. You'll either adapt and survive or you won't.

It's also a huge opportunity, because if you keep doing things the same way you've always done them or propping up the status quo, you'll burn out.

I know this because I've lived it.

I want you to have the opportunity to learn from the biggest mistake I've made in my career.

It was about eight years ago when I was working in a senior role in a fast-paced, global corporation. I really loved my job. I thought I had everything under control. I spent a lot of time with my husband, James, and our children, who were six and four at the time, and I felt like I was doing a good job at leading my team. I ran three times a week. I did yoga once a week. I caught up with my friends on a regular basis. I had balance, despite the demands of my intense corporate job.

One day, the CEO asked me to take on a special project in addition to my normal responsibilities. I saw it as a great opportunity to learn from him, so I was super excited to take on the project. And it was going to be great for my career. Why would I turn it down?

Burnout doesn't happen straight away. It took me about three months.

At night, I'd put the kids to bed, open my laptop, and sit on the couch to get some extra work done. At about 10 p.m., I'd clear out my email inbox. I'd work until midnight to try to get on top of things. I wanted to feel like I was in control. At 6 a.m., I'd get up, do what I needed to do to take care of the kids, and start my workday again.

At the end of each day, I'd take a look at my workload and make a decision. Do I go for a run or get more work done? Do I do yoga or do more work? Each time, I chose work. Even when it came to sleep, work won. After that, other bad habits crept in.

I'd pick the kids up from school and day care, go home, and start thinking about what to make for dinner. Because I usually hadn't given it any consideration beforehand, I'd look for the easiest option. And I ended up on this downward spiral until one weekend, when I knew I wasn't well. On the Sunday night, I opened my work laptop. I stared at my calendar, with the goal to figure out when I could take a sick day that week. I thought a day off was all that was needed to make me feel better and then I'd be back to 100 percent.

But as I stared at my calendar, all I could see was important meetings. Every day. Monday through Friday was filled with important meetings, which left me no time for a day off to get better.

So on the Monday, I simply showed up at the office for work. I was coughing and fighting fatigue, but I pushed through. By Wednesday, my cough was sounding like a barking dog. I just kept pushing. I was focused on getting to Saturday, thinking that would be my day to recharge. But on Friday, while meeting with my boss, he said, "Tina, are you OK?" He was genuinely concerned.

I paused, took a deep breath, and said, "No. I'm not."

I knew we were in an important meeting, but I couldn't function properly. I had to leave right then. I packed up my things and went straight to my doctor. Within five minutes, he sent me to the emergency department of my local hospital, where they diagnosed me with pneumonia. I had worked all week with pneumonia.

As I lay there in the emergency department with James now by my side, I kept apologizing. I kept saying to him, "I tried to be strong and push through." I'll never forget what he said to me.

"Tina, no job is ever worth you lying here in the emergency department."

Of course, I knew he was right. No job was worth being so sick that I needed that many painkillers and antibiotics running through me. But I didn't know how to fix my problem.

I had prioritized everyone else over myself. My husband, my kids, my team, my stakeholders, my boss. My health came last. And while lying there in the emergency department, I thought, *I'm not being a great leader for my team. I'm not being a great role model for them. I'm not being a great employee. I'm not being a great wife. Or a great parent.* I hadn't returned any of my friends' phone calls, so I thought, *I'm not even being a great friend.* I was putting everyone else first.

James had called his parents to look after our kids so that he could be at the hospital with me. I felt like I was letting everyone down. The reality was, I had let myself down. That wasn't the life I wanted. I didn't want to be so exhausted that I needed the emergency department.

Telling this story now reminds me of the proverbial frog in the pot of boiling water. If you put the frog in the water while it's boiling, it immediately jumps out. But if you put it in cold water and turn up the heat slowly, then it doesn't realize it's too hot until it's too late. I was the frog and the pressure I had put myself under was the water with the heat slowly turned up.

I'd been making micro-decisions, focused on work instead of myself, and that led to a serious burnout.

After taking a month to recover, I realized that I wanted a different life for me and my family. Even though I loved my corporate job and I wanted to continue to have a wonderful career, I had to make changes. I analyzed my old habits in detail and sprung into action. I took the time to look for every article, video, and piece of information I could find on how to have a successful corporate career AND a life outside of work. For me, that meant having a strong marriage and raising our kids aligned with our values. It also included yoga, running, giving back, traveling and many other activities associated with an active and meaningful life.

However, I became really frustrated, because all the advice I came across said the same thing. *You've got to fit your own oxygen mask first.*

It was an analogy. Like being on a plane where there's an emergency, they always tell you to fit your own oxygen mask before you help someone else fit theirs. In other words, they were telling me that I couldn't lead my team effectively or care for anyone else if I wasn't taking care of myself. I got annoyed because I agreed with them. It made sense. However, every article, book, and video fell short of telling me *how* to do it.

I knew I needed to look after myself, but I didn't know how. When I had back-to-back meetings from 8 a.m. to 5 p.m. and my "real work" started at five, when I had to pick up the kids, make dinner, and try to get eight hours of sleep, that seemed like an impossible task. How could I fit it all into twenty-four hours? So, I went on this journey of discovery, experimenting with different work, productivity and well-being hacks. I read everything I could find on the subject, to find out the secret to this thing called work-life balance. I wanted to know what actually works for a leader in a fast-paced company, not just the theories.

Every time I found a nugget, something I wanted to experiment with, I'd ask myself, "Could this work for me? Could I apply this to my role as a senior leader in a large, global company?"

I wanted to work out which tips were practical, realistic, and sustainable. To do this, I'd try them on myself, and check to make sure they stuck over time.

Once I started seeing results, I started teaching my teams, colleagues, and mentees how to apply them too.

In parallel, I knew my leadership style was different from most other corporate leaders. I'd led my teams for several years with the mantra, "Outcomes over hours in the office." My team knew that I didn't care when or where they worked, as long as they collaborated effectively to get their most valuable work done. Way before "remote teams," "hybrid teams," "virtual teams," and "distributed teams" were phrases common in today's corporate language, my teams worked in this way. We worked out together what was needed to make this way of working … well, work.

And this is what I now teach to leadership teams in other large, global organizations.

One of the things leaders tell me is how practical my strategies are. The reason they're so practical is that they've been tried and tested by leaders who've been in similar situations as them. Armed with my twenty-plus years of theory, practice, and experimentation, I'm ready to write and publish the first manual with tried and tested tips on how to effectively lead remote teams.

In this book, I will share with you the success stories of some of my clients, the words of wisdom from progressive corporate executives who I have interviewed, and relevant details from my own story. The leaders I've coached who have implemented these strategies are more productive, happier, and healthier as a result. Twenty-five percent more, in fact.[1] And I implemented these strategies myself without dialing back my ambition. If they can work for me, they can work for you too.

There's nothing about the strategies I share that requires any leader to scale back on productivity. Far from it! When I first started my journey post burnout, I thought I had to choose between being productive at work or being healthy. I had experienced a lot of major achievements. I had worked hard to

---

1 - Results come from analyzing the pre- and post-program results of my clients' leadership teams that have gone through my signature "Outcomes Over Hours" Group Coaching Program.

have a successful corporate career. And I had a family and other things outside of work that were very important to me too. I thought I had to choose between them. But I didn't.

There's a great concept known as The Four Burners Theory. Think of yourself as a stove with four burners. There's your work, your family, your friends, and your health. The theory goes that "in order to be successful you have to cut off one of your burners. And in order to be really successful you have to cut off two."[2] In other words, you can't go gung-ho on all four burners through your entire life. Or if you try, the health burner will go off. You'll burn out.

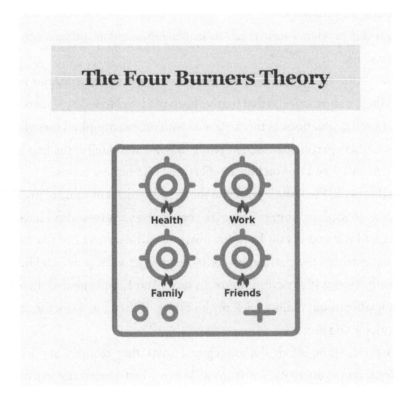

I agree with this concept but with one big caveat: There are ways you can have more heat on all the burners you want to at the same time if you do it

2 - *"The Downside of Work-Life Balance,"* James Clear.

consciously. I didn't want to have to choose between them, so I had to figure out how I was going to make it work.

I knew I could do it. I had built a career on transformation, building systems and processes for large corporate teams. Certainly, I could build a system for four burners.

My experience as a former director of business transformation programs makes me uniquely qualified to teach my strategies and systems, and apply them to a variety of situations, for leaders who feel so busy, yet want to be more productive and stay healthy. I've done it and I've now helped thousands of other corporate leaders across six continents to do it too.

As a certified Master Black Belt in Lean Six Sigma, I've been trained over the past two decades in process improvement disciplines. I took the Lean Six Sigma methodologies and started with defining the problem. My problem was simple: I wanted to thrive in my corporate career leading large teams, while also focusing on the people and things of value to me outside of work. And, of course, my health.

The key principle when analyzing the current state of any process is to work out which parts of the process have value. Which parts will the customer pay for? And which parts are value-enabling, such as meeting regulatory requirements, or are absolutely necessary for the value-added parts to happen?

Then there are the parts of a process that don't actually add value to the customer, even though they might appear like they do on the surface. These things are known as "non-value adds." Often, these are things that might have made sense a long time ago or are workarounds for a poorly designed process. We often keep these steps in our processes because we don't take the time to think through if we really need them. We don't stop and consciously reflect on if they add value for our team, our customers, or our organization. I adapted this way of thinking and made it relevant for me. I looked at my life in totality and asked myself,

What adds value?

What is value-enabling?

What is a non-value add?

When I thought about it, I realized that coaching my team drove immense value. When I had meetings with key executives to discuss my team's progress and outcomes so they could trust them and help remove any roadblocks, that was a value-added activity. When my team delivered features that made things better for our end customers, that was value-added work.

In a different area of my life, I realized that brushing my teeth every morning and night was value-enabling. It was not an activity that directly added significant value that day, but it was something with cumulative impact. So I identified the things in my life that weren't directly adding significant value that day but still made sense to be included for my overall productivity, health, and happiness.

Once I identified my value-enabling activities, I asked myself which ones I could combine. Things like running while listening to a podcast. I evaluated what activities I was doing regularly and asked myself if it was a value-added, value-enabling, or non-value-added task. Then I'd pair up my value-enabling activities with value-added activities where I could. I started doing twenty squats while waiting for my morning coffee to brew (which is completely a value-add activity in my life!). I would alternate running to and from work, combining my physical fitness with commuting to the office.

I measured and then analyzed the "current state" of my life to then improve it. When I measured my current state, I realized how much time I wasted on activities that were a non-value add. Attending meetings where I really didn't need to be there. Writing long responses to emails when one or two lines would have sufficed. Intending to scroll through social media for five minutes, only to still be on my phone two hours later watching cat videos. Things that didn't help me focus on what was important in my work and life.

Bottom line, I took a structured approach to solving my own problem, using the skills I had developed in business.

I also adopted various Agile practices.

Agile has become increasingly popular in many global organizations over the past twenty or so years. Agile is not about having everything perfectly designed and then building it. Rather, it's about iterating, experimenting, testing, and learning. For me, I started treating my life as one big experiment and made improvements as I went. I evaluated every new strategy I implemented to learn what worked and what didn't. Over time, what didn't work got discarded. I kept iterating until I could improve it at scale.

I've seen first-hand the impact these strategies have had on my teams and me. We've been able to get more valuable work done AND have more freedom to focus on what matters to each of us outside of work. My teams knew that I trusted them. I'd tell them, "I don't care when you work, and I don't care where you work, as long as you can collaborate effectively to get the right outcomes done."

Practically speaking, this meant most team members were usually in the office, but had the freedom to work from home (or elsewhere) when it suited them. Built on a foundation of trust, they organized their days around when it made sense to be in the office. For example, to sit face-to-face with a coworker when they had to have a difficult conversation. Often they would prioritize being in the office when they had a complex workshop to facilitate, which involved putting Post-it Notes up on the walls of the office to work through project timings and issues. When it made sense to be in the office based on the type of work they had planned for that day, they were in the office. When it made sense to work from home or elsewhere, they worked from outside the office. I would communicate and recommunicate that the most important thing to me was to collaborate effectively so we could deliver the most valuable outcomes for our people, our customers, and our organization. It was up to them where that happened.

Giving my team this freedom paid me back in spades. One of them said to me one day, "I've never been so motivated to work so hard for a leader before. I just didn't want to let you down since you gave me so much flexibility to do my job on my terms."

I trusted her. She was an outstanding talent in the organization, so why wouldn't I? I remember the day when her son received an award in his school assembly. It was at 12:30 p.m.—which didn't fit nicely with being in the office in the city from 9 a.m. to 5 p.m.—so she simply worked from home that day. She walked the four blocks from her home to the school to see him get his award, then walked home and kept working. She had never had that opportunity before. I know that day, having the permission to work from home AND to focus on what mattered to her outside of work, she continued to deliver on all her work outcomes. Like she always did.

Clear expectations are key to leading a high-performing remote team. The team knows working from anywhere is not an opportunity for them to put their feet up and watch TV all day. They know they must still deliver top-notch, first-class outcomes and value.

They're grown-ups. It's up to them to choose how long they'll work each day. I know that I don't do my best work when somebody's looking over my shoulder. I passed that philosophy on to my team to show them that I trusted them to do their work. When something slipped through the cracks, we'd have a conversation about it because I still expected excellence. But they got to work more on their own terms. They knew, and I knew, that what they did outside of work had a massive impact on their attitude, their mindset, and their productivity while working.

I've spent more than two decades working in the corporate world, which has prepared me to write this book. First working in senior roles across nine industries and twelve countries, where I led departments of hundreds of people, governed billions of dollars worth of assets, and my teams delivered programs and projects worth hundreds of millions of dollars. Pre-COVID, I started my own business teaching leadership teams in the corporate world across six continents how to get their work done effectively and look after themselves and their teams. My signature program, "Outcomes Over Hours," teaches leaders how to get their most valuable work done effectively and frees them and their teams up to do their work when and where they work best.

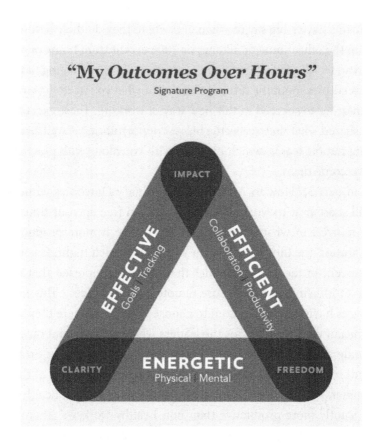

In part 1, "How to Lead Yourself," I'll share with you some of the practical strategies so you can give yourself permission to look after yourself—and know that it won't be at the cost of having a successful career.

In part 2, "How to Lead Your Teams," I will go deep on the leadership skills and capabilities you will need to succeed as a leader whose team members are not always in the same location as each other and you. There are several terms you've probably heard to describe teams that do not work together in the same location (typically an office) and during similar hours 100 percent of the time. "Remote," "virtual," "distributed," and "hybrid" (where you spend a portion of your time working in the office and the rest from elsewhere) all describe teams that are not all working 100 percent in the same place and at the same time. To keep things simple, I consistently use the term "remote" throughout the book. Remote teams have a big say in when and where they do their best work. This could be in the office some or all days or 100 percent from home or elsewhere. You will read words of wisdom from progressive CEOs, managing partners and C-suite executives about the future of work and what you need to start working on now in order to succeed in this new way of working. These executives have candidly shared what they see as the biggest opportunities as well as challenges for leading remote teams, which I'll share with you along with practical strategies to overcome them.

And in part 3, "How to Achieve Extraordinary Outcomes without Burnout," I will share how to work smarter, so you can free up your time and your teams to reinvest in what really matters to you, be it more productive work or being around the dinner table with your family each night. Gartner found that 74 percent of the 317 companies they surveyed reported that they were intending to indefinitely adopt more remote work practices.[3] This new norm, of employees having more freedom to choose when and where they work, creates significant opportunities for the leaders who choose to embrace it. When leaders understand that empowering their people to work more on their own terms leads to better work outcomes, they also reap the benefits of their teams being happier, healthier, and even more productive.[4] In fact, healthy workers are significantly more productive than non-healthy workers.[5] There's a pretty good return on investment to give people the freedom to work on their own terms and look after themselves.

As I write this chapter, I'm looking out over the ocean about two hours away from my home in Melbourne, Australia. This is where James and I are working reduced hours over the next two weeks during the school holidays with our kids. Still embodying my mantra, *"Outcomes over hours in the office,"* two decades on has been one of the best decisions I've made in my life. I hope it is for you too.

---

3 - Gartner, April 2020.

4 - *Remote Work Revolution* by Tsedal Neeley.

5 - *Wall Street Journal*, Lauren Weber, 2017, https://www.wsj.com/articles/ healthy-workers-are-more-productive-study-finds-1502219651.

CHAPTER 2

Press Pause

"When we press the pause button on a machine, it stops. But when we press the pause buttons on human beings, they start."
—Dov Seidman

These days, we're constantly go, go, go.

It reminds me of a cartoon I read as a kid where cavemen were pushing a cart with square wheels. Another character stood off to the side with round wheels in hand, asking, "Can I help?" The ones pushing the cart shrugged him off.

"No, we're too busy," they said.

That's sort of what many leaders do today at work. They keep doing the same things they've always done, but don't reflect on how their environment might have changed and, therefore, ways they might now need to act differently. They're resigned to putting in loads of time and effort pushing square wheels. If they could pause and consider alternative ways to accomplish things, they'd find the round wheels that would get them to where they want to go faster. They'd be more effective and efficient.

Most of us don't take the time to pause and look around for the round wheels, so we keep going with those clunky old square wheels. There's the old saying, usually attributed to Albert Einstein, "Insanity is doing the same thing over and over again expecting different results." It's true.

The key to getting different (better) results is to press pause. The key is to consciously reflect on, analyze, and think through what is currently working for you and your team and what isn't.

It's not about redoing everything. In most cases, we're not just hitting reset and starting over. It's a pause. Time for reflection.

When we don't press pause, over time, it can lead to us only seeing one step in front of us because we're in "survival mode." We simply keep doing things the way we've always done them, because the thought of trying something new is simply, well, exhausting. This is when flipping the pause switch is most necessary. It allows us to expand our consciousness and actually think through if there's a better way of doing things.

A fight-or-flight mechanism was necessary for our survival in the primitive stages of our evolution. If you encountered a wild animal, this mechanism came in handy to escape or fight it off. It was a major determinant in whether you were going to have steak for dinner or if you were going to be steak for dinner. In our current high-technology always-on environment, it's not as necessary to constantly be in this heightened state these days for survival. A clear head and a calmer state are much better mechanisms for survival today in the corporate world.

When I coach leaders to press pause, I ask them to think about who of the following three people they relate to the most. Person A is the legendary Wim Hof, also known as "The Iceman." Wim consistently stays calm, focused, and in control despite often being in incredibly challenging external circumstances. At last count, Wim has twenty-six Guinness World Records. He's climbed Mount Everest in his shorts. He's developed millions of followers around the world for his unique breathing and meditation techniques to help people remain calm and focused, despite the challenges they might face day to day. Wim Hof demonstrates that when external circumstances are challenging, when things get tough, you can still feel strong and in control. You don't let your external environment dictate your state of mind.

You might relate more to Person B: a synchronized swimmer. You often have a big smile on your face and look cool, calm, and collected on the surface, but below the water, you are kicking like mad just to keep it all together. Everyone else sees the calm, but you are working so hard mentally and physically where others can't see what it's taking to make it happen.

Or you might relate more to Person C: a passenger on the *Titanic*. You feel overwhelmed, exhausted. Like you're drowning. You know you're not in a good state, but you don't really know what to do to get yourself out of it.

When I present these three scenarios to leaders around the world, very few say they feel like Wim Hof. Most don't feel in control. They don't feel strong in the situation they've found themselves in. They're constantly trying to juggle their workload and life outside work. Most tell me they feel like the synchronized swimmer. They are fighting so hard behind the scenes to keep it all together. And a significant number admit they oscillate between being that synchronized swimmer and feeling like a passenger on the *Titanic*. It can often only take a few really small things not going right for them to move pretty quickly from being a Person B to a Person C.

When I discuss this concept with leaders, I tell them that wherever they are today, it's not static. If they feel like a Person B or C right now, there are practical things they can do to move up, over time, to being a Person A. But you must know where you are today so you can focus on where you want to be tomorrow. It's not a set-and-forget tactic. It's something to reflect on continually and get better at over time. When I think back to my own burnout story, I was generally a Person A before my burnout. Most weeks, I felt like Wim Hof, before I took on the special project that did me in. Over time though, I stopped doing the things that made me feel strong and in control. Running, yoga, getting sufficient sleep, and eating healthy meals. That's when I slid down the slippery slope to being like a synchronized swimmer and eventually like a passenger on the *Titanic*.

I encourage you to get in the habit of pressing pause and checking your work pulse regularly. Do you feel like Wim Hof today? Do you feel like a synchronized swimmer? Or are you starting down that slippery slope toward feeling like a passenger on the *Titanic*?

Identify where you are right now so that you can give yourself your best chance of feeling like Wim in the long term.

The "always-on" culture

71% adults sleep with their phone in reach

41% are woken at night by notifications

12% deliberately wake to use their phone

85% reach for their phone when they wake up

50% take their phone to the toilet[6]

I started my corporate career back in 1999. We had email, but we didn't have smartphones. Most people would work all day in the office from Monday to Friday. At the end of the workday, when we closed our computers at our desks in the office, we'd typically go home and sleep well at night. Because we didn't have smartphones, we would often go home and cook dinner, play cards, watch some TV, and wake up at a reasonable hour in the morning, ready to go into the office again. Now, many people have your phone number programmed into their phone and they can contact you at any hour of the day. We constantly have our phones with us. Not only can others readily contact you, but they have several different ways to contact you—be it by phone call, text, work messaging channels, social media profiles—the list goes on.

Many corporate leaders I coach have ten or more different ways they can be reached. Having so many different ways you can be contacted can be exhausting, and when set up with no boundaries, it effectively means you have an open-door policy 24-7.

---

6 - *Life Mode On* by Dr. Joanne Orlando

If you're the kind of leader who is used to always being there for everyone else, that means you're always "on." It doesn't stop at 5 p.m. Most of us check in with our phones as the last thing we do before going to bed at night. Then we check again first thing in the morning. As mentioned, 71 percent of adults sleep with their phone within arm's reach. Eighty-five percent reach for their phone first thing in the morning. The average adult checks their phone seventy-six times a day.[7]

If you're working on a task and your phone pings and you look at it, it breaks your concentration. Even if it's just for three seconds to read a message, now you have to get back into the flow of your original task. It takes time to get back to the same level of concentration. Studies show that it takes an average of twenty-three minutes and fifteen seconds to get back to the same level of deep work.[8] Now imagine your phone pinging a hundred times a day.

What most leaders focus on is that three seconds. They'll tell themselves, "I only looked away from my work for three seconds, so I was unproductive for just three seconds. No harm done." But those three seconds aren't the problem. The real problem is it breaking your concentration and the resulting twenty-three minutes it takes for you to fully focus again. Taking time to press pause helps you reflect and look for those round wheels.

Rushing from meeting to meeting, constantly checking your phone, being "always-on" ... it's exhausting. And it's counterintuitive to being productive. You're training your brain to be reactive and less productive. Over time, your brain will adapt to being reactive and lead to you focusing your time and effort where others want you versus proactively focusing on what actually adds the most value. Every time you get pinged or receive a notification, it's tempting to look because it releases dopamine into your brain. It's something new. A novelty. A new high. And you connect with someone so your brain releases oxytocin, the bonding hormone. That's why people can easily get addicted to

---

7 - *Life Mode On* by Dr. Joanne Orlando.

8 - "Worker, Interrupted: The Cost of Task Switching," Kermit Pattison.

social media. And the end result is an inability to be proactive, because the brain rewires to the reactive environment, the "always-on" culture.

These pings on your phone, your email, your social media, those may not be the things that are going to help you or your team the most. Checking on all of those pings and responding every time you get one typically leads to a delusion of progress. If you pause, you can ask yourself, "Is this my most valuable work?" "Is this the most valuable activity for me to be doing right now?"

Momentum is a great thing, but it can also be a facade. You might feel like you're progressing your outcomes and doing meaningful work based on your busy activity, but being busy doesn't always show up as value for your customers, employees, or organization. That's a delusion of progress.

While in that hospital bed in the emergency department with pneumonia, if someone had said to me, "Tina, you need to press pause," my thought process at the time would have been, "I just need to double down and work a bit harder!"

I loved my work. I wanted to do it well. And I felt like I was busy, getting things done and rushing from meeting to meeting. In my mind, that's what it took to do a great job and be an effective leader.

Fifteen years ago, I got some great feedback from a boss. I wish I had really listened to her then. During my performance appraisal, she said, "The key thing I want you to learn is to be still. I want you to be able to have two hours in your calendar each day where you don't have meetings, where you're not rushing around, where you're just sitting. You're thinking, reflecting, creating, innovating."

She told me that's typically when the great ideas come. Those are the times when you think of ways to do things differently. There are icons of the business world who have worked this way for years. Think Warren Buffett and Bill Gates.

I didn't immediately follow her advice at the time because I thought two hours a day of just sitting and thinking made no sense. I dismissed it. Fast forward to a few years later and I faced a tricky business problem while leading a large operations department. I needed to reduce my department's costs. I was told that the easiest way for me to do this would be to get my employees in the contact center to spend less time on the phone talking with customers, because that would help bring our costs down. That didn't make sense to me though, because I wanted my team to speak with our customers for as long as they needed to in order to resolve their queries. I couldn't see an alternative solution, however, as I rushed about my days. Then I was selected to attend a special leadership conference in Beijing, China. While away from the busyness of the office and the day-to-day issues, I was listening to a speaker on a different topic altogether. I pulled out a piece of paper and started scribbling some notes.

I let my mind wander. I started to brainstorm the things that were in my control regarding my department's costs. I wrote a few things down and realized that the number of calls that came into the contact center had a big impact on how many employees I needed on the phones at a given time—and therefore had a massive impact on my department's budget. This was something I could somewhat control. I could work out why our customers were calling us and fix our processes so that they didn't have to call us multiple times for the same reason. I also instinctively knew this would improve the overall customer experience, because it's a rare person who likes calling a contact center to resolve an issue during their lunch break. When I got back from Beijing, we kicked off a new initiative based on that brainstorming session and called it "First Call Resolution."

The idea was to focus on the customer and why they were calling us. I wasn't addressing how much time my team spent talking to customers on the phone. Instead, we asked why the customer was calling us. Our focus turned to fixing the customers' problems so that they didn't have to call us multiple times.

Sitting and thinking, pressing pause, led me to this idea that was revolutionary at the time (it was many years ago!). The outcome was that we relatively easily then addressed our budget issues, while simulatneously improving the customer experience. Pressing pause works.

The three lenses of value

As a leader, I started to obsessively focus on my three lenses of value:

1. What can I do to drive more value for our customers?
2. What can I do to drive more value for our organization?
3. What can I do to add more value for my team, so that they can in turn drive more value for our customers and organization?

Working smarter, not harder, is shifting the focus from how many hours you work and how many emails you've answered to what matters most to your people, your customers, and your organization. Flipping the script from inputs to outputs.

One of my role models, the late Edward de Bono, who coined the term "lateral thinking," exemplifies the "work smarter, not harder" mantra. He pioneered "thinking outside the box" and encouraged companies to do so, as well. In his book *Serious Creativity*, he writes how he was told by his publisher that his book draft wouldn't be taken seriously because it wasn't long enough. They said it needed to be at least a couple of hundred pages long. So, not by preference, he padded out the book with more pages, openly writing about how he added in extra pages so people would feel they got value buying his book— even though he felt the key concepts could be communicated to the reader in far fewer pages. In a similar way, many business leaders have this notion that quantity is the thing that matters most, when it's quality that really matters.

The Three Lenses of Value

1. What can I do to drive more value for our customers?

2. What can I do to drive more value for our organization?

3. What can I do to drive more value for my team, so that they can in turn drive more value for our customers and organization?

Just like the three lenses of value perspective I use to determine where to spend my time, I use three lenses for how to interact with information on social media. This approach comes from the parenting expert Dr. Justin Coulson. Consider your own social media use through the lenses of the three Cs:

1. Connecting: Interacting with friends and family from around the world can be a wonderful thing and one of the benefits of social media.

2. Creating: Are you contributing new ideas into the world or learning new concepts that will help you create a better life for yourself? Creating is another great use of social media that can have real benefits.

3. Consuming: This is the one that is usually the big time suck. Are you consuming for the sake of consuming? Think cat videos and the like here. Is this how you want to spend large amounts of your time if you're feeling overwhelmed? We all need our downtime, but consider whether you want to spend five minutes consuming

or five hours. In business and in life, it's important to think about connecting, creating, and consuming. Why are you doing what you're doing and is it the best use of your time?

Just to be clear, I'm not a robot! I love having downtime—time when I'm doing nothing but consuming. Watching sitcoms on the couch with my family is time well spent in my book. However, I'm mindful of my time ratio. Binge-watch your favorite TV show if it's something that makes you happy, but be conscious of the ratio of time you spend in those three Cs of connecting, creating, and consuming. If you spend more time consuming than connecting or creating, maybe consider if there's an imbalance you want to address. You're a grown-up—it's about consciously settling on a ratio that works for you.

The water you carry

We tend to put our various roles on a shelf. We play them one by one, task switching from one to another. Now I'm a worker, now I'm a leader, now I'm a mentor, a spouse, a partner, a parent, a child. We don't think about them all running concurrently. Thanks to Marty Linsky for the original concept and to Gabrielle Dolan who shared it with me.

Imagine that you are carrying a bucket of water on your head, filled with water for each of the roles you play in your life that take up your time and energy. The more time and energy a role takes up in your life, the more water that gets added to your imaginary bucket that weighs you down.

Write down all the roles you play in your life. What roles do you play at work? At home? In the community?

Given you're reading this book, an employee is probably one for you. Leader probably is too. You could be a mentor to emerging talent in your organization. You might have been assigned to a special project on top of your day job, like I was when I burned out. You could be the subject matter expert, the go-to person, for a specific type of technology used a lot in your organization. You might be a trusted colleague who many employees confide in. A quasi-therapist when your team members are dealing with major issues. You may have more roles at work that come to mind for you.

Outside of work, you could be a spouse or partner. Or a parent. You may have other dependents you care for, such as elderly parents or siblings. You might be a confidante to friends. A neighbor. Maybe you're on a committee at your child's school. You could be a volunteer at a nonprofit. Maybe you're an athlete (however loosely you define that!) and part of a sporting team. Again, there are so many roles you could play in your life that don't involve your work.

When I first went through this exercise, I had more than twenty roles I was playing inside and outside of work. No wonder I felt so exhausted!

Take a clean sheet of paper and draw a circle for each role you play, whether it be at work or outside of work. Make the size of the circle based on how much water you're carrying in that role. If it requires a lot of time and energy, draw a bigger circle. If it doesn't take up much time or energy, make the circle smaller. When I first did this exercise, the special project I was leading was a big circle. Being a leader was a big circle. Being an employee was a big circle. Being a parent was a big circle. Yet, I'd kept all my other circles at the same size when I took on that special project. Nothing was deprioritized. By not reassessing and then readjusting all the roles I played, something had to give. And in the end, that was my health.

Working through which roles drain you and which ones give you energy can help you see if and where you're feeling overwhelmed. Two practical questions to ask yourself are, "Where am I carrying too much water?" and "Where might I be carrying someone else's water?"

One client of mine who went through this exercise said, "Wow! I'm the one doing so much on this project that everyone is supposed to be doing together, with equal responsibilities. But I feel like I'm carrying all the water."

We then workshopped a conversation he knew he needed to have to discuss how to redistribute the responsibilities. Empty some of that water from his bucket.

While you're carrying your bucket, if some water spills, and it will, don't always be the first to reach for the mop! Your role is not to save everyone else and do their work for them. Of course, it's essential to be there when the people in your life need you and you don't want critical tasks at work to fall through the cracks. However, be conscious about how you might be enabling others.

About a year ago, after explaining the water you carry concept to an operations leadership team, a wonderful man said to me, "Tina, I'm a bit embarrassed and somewhat ashamed, but I need to share with the team what's going through my mind." He said, "You're talking about analyzing where we're carrying too much water, as shown by the big circles versus the small circles for the roles we play. However, I've just realized I've got this really small circle for the role of spouse and another really small circle for the role of parent. I know if my wife were here doing this exercise, her page would be filled with huge circles. I'm not carrying enough water. I need to step up with my family."

He recognized that the water he was carrying in his roles at work involved a lot of his time and energy, but his roles outside of work didn't. He wasn't giving those priority, which was impacting his relationships outside work.

That resonated with a lot of his peers on the call. And when I share this story with others in my group coaching programs, many say, "I get it. I'm in a similar situation."

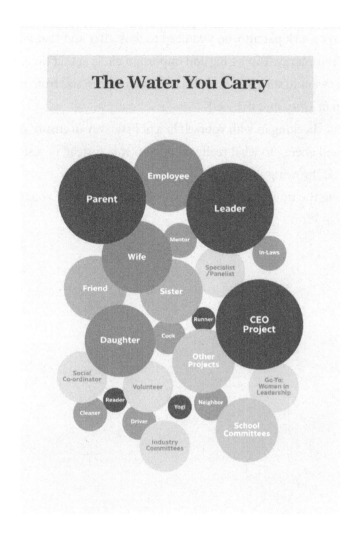

This is what mine looked like just before I burned out.

One other point about your responsibilities involves your roles where you have drawn big circles. I'm not saying you must invest less in those circles. Your role as a leader is probably a big circle. If so, it's not necessary to shrink it. The exercise is simply to help you be aware of where your obligations are in totality and to consciously assess whether you're spending the right amount of time and energy on each role when you assess them all together.

Your roles and responsibilities are not static. They're dynamic. One year, you may have a sick parent who you need to look after and that may require a lot of time and energy. That's a big and important circle at that time. You probably wouldn't want to shrink it. Your circles can change in size from time to time, as well as in priority, and that's OK.

It's about checking in with yourself in a holistic way to ensure you're giving your time and energy to what really matters to you, instead of just responding to what life is throwing at you.

By taking the time to press pause, you're giving yourself your best shot to feel more like Wim.

CHAPTER 3

Making Habits Stick

"Easy choices, hard life. Hard choices, easy life."
—Jerzy Gregorek

We all know we should eat our broccoli. Most people know that having a lot of fruit and vegetables in their diet means they're going to be healthier. Fruit and vegetables help us live longer and they build up our immune system. Yet, only 10 percent eat the recommended servings of fruits and vegetables each day.[9]

One of the things I've realized is that knowledge is usually not enough to make good habits stick. Knowledge is a good beginning, but it doesn't build sustainable habits. We need to look at our behaviors, examine our commitment levels, and execute on a planned course of action to change them if we want to build sustainable habits. One thing I stress to clients when working through the "press pause" exercise as to whether they feel like Wim Hof, a synchronized swimmer, or a passenger on the *Titanic* is to do this quick sense-check regularly. How you feel can change over time. You might feel like Wim Hof one month and the next month a passenger on the *Titanic*.

It's relatively easy to slip into bad habits, even when you've been doing well. Whether it's getting enough sleep, eating well, exercising, or being disciplined

9 - Centers for Disease Control and Prevention, 2017: https://www.cdc.gov/media/releases/2017/p1116-fruit-vegetable-consumption.html.

with your social media, it doesn't take much to slip into bad habits. That's why constantly having the press pause exercise front of mind and knowing that you're never done—that we are always a work in progress—is an important mindset. This isn't a set-and-forget activity.

Nudges

That said, you can "nudge" yourself to make your habits stick. Chip and Dan Heath coined this term in their excellent book *Switch: How to Change Things When Change Is Hard.* Another great read in this space is Charles Duhigg's *The Power of Habit: Why We Do What We Do in Life and Business.* Nudges are like little processes or automations you put in place to "nudge" you toward the behavior you want to sustain. Examples include laying out your running clothes the night before, going food shopping when you're full so you don't just buy whatever unhealthy foods look good, or charging your phone in another room so you don't keep scrolling when it's time for sleep.

The whole idea is to be conscious of the habits you want to develop and knowing that most of us get the wobbles when it comes to consistently doing the right thing. Relying on motivation alone is not the best way to go. As a chief financial officer (CFO) I worked with used to say, "Hope is not a strategy." In terms of motivating yourself to change your habits, hope is not enough to make them consistently happen.

Michelle Bridges is an amazing fitness expert in Australia. She's known as the epitome of health, someone who goes out for hour-long runs frequently. She's also known as someone who is always full of energy. Many people presume she's just lucky to always feel motivated to exercise. I recently heard her speak, where the gist of what she said was, *I'm not motivated every morning to go for a run. But I know the benefits of running and, because of that, put systems in place to make sure it happens. If you wait for your motivation to come before you do these things, you'll be waiting a very long time.*

Once you have the knowledge, how do you make good habits stick? Take your thinking out of your head. In other words, systemize your behaviors to make them a part of your regular routine.

There's a wonderful book called *How to Change: The Science of Getting from Where You Are to Where You Want to Be* by Katy Milkman. In her book, Milkman discusses how to set up your system to help you swap bad habits for good habits. When I say "system," this often means calendar. One of the top reasons people don't follow through on changing their habits is that they simply forget. They don't set out to fail. Whether we're talking about completing a work task or going for a walk, they just forget to do it because it wasn't on their radar. They didn't systematize it.

If it's important to you, put it in your calendar.

Whether it's running, Pilates, or dropping your kids at school, you've got to schedule it in. It's the same thing with reminders. Whether you're writing your daily to-do list or wanting to meditate for ten minutes a day, you need a system to remind you to do it. This could be booking a fifteen-minute meeting with yourself in your calendar. It could be setting an alarm on your phone for 5 p.m. each workday to remind you to write out your task list for tomorrow. Whatever it is, where possible, automate it so you don't have to rely on you simply remembering to do it.

Nudges are also great to remind you to move about during the day, particularly if you sit at your desk for the bulk of the day. You might have heard the phrase "Sitting is the new smoking." As Gavin Bradley described in an interview for the *Washington Post*:

"Metabolism slows down 90 percent after thirty minutes of sitting. The enzymes that move the bad fat from your arteries to your muscles, where it can get burned off, slow down. And after two hours, good cholesterol drops 20 percent. Just getting up for five minutes is going to get things going again. These things are so simple they're almost stupid."[10]

---

10 - *Ikagi: The Japanese Secret to a Long and Happy Life* by Hector Garcia and Francesc Miralles.

When people work from home, they are often sedentary for hours at a time. In the office, you might be in meetings throughout the day, and walking from one meeting room to another. You're not at your desk all day. You walk a flight of stairs to attend a meeting, then an hour or two later, you walk down again. Then you walk to the café down the street for lunch. You get a lot of incidental exercise that you don't typically get when you're working from home.

Working from home, all the meetings happen in the same place. You simply click the link to start your video call and a different button to end the call. All while walking zero steps.

Set one of your devices to alert you to take a five-minute stretch break every hour. Scheduling meetings for twenty-five minutes instead of thirty can also nudge you to make the time to stretch or take a break.

Another simple nudge: In the morning, instead of having your alarm clock next to your bed where you can hit the snooze button and roll over, place it a few feet away so that you must get out of bed to turn off the alarm. Once you're out of bed, you're more likely to start your day. A simple yet effective nudge.

Spend a few minutes now to think through what nudges could help you to create good and sustainable habits. Taking time now to identify and implement your own nudges will give you a much better shot at making them sustainable.

"Habit stacking" is another practical strategy. This concept comes from James Clear, who wrote the super practical book *Atomic Habits: An Easy and Proven Way to Build Good Habits and Break Bad Ones*. He invites readers to think about the habits they practice every day without thinking about them. For most people, that includes brushing your teeth twice a day. For people who do that, they typically brush their teeth in the morning after breakfast and then brush them again at night before going to bed. You probably have habits that you have ingrained into yourself. Things you've done since you were a child. Habit stacking is pairing new habits with those ingrained habits, so that you can include them in your daily routine. It helps put you on autopilot to remember to do your new good habits.

One habit stacking nudge that helps me drink over eight glasses of water each day comes from Cameron Diaz's book *The Body Book: The Law of Hunger, The Science of Strength, and Other Ways to Love Your Amazing Body*. I have a big glass bottle sitting next to my toothbrush that I fill with water. Right before I brush my teeth in the morning, I drink the bottle of water and immediately refill it.

At the end of the day, I drink another half of that bottle of water, just before I brush my teeth (I don't want to drink too much water right before going to bed!). I then fill the bottle back up to the top. This way, I get about half of my daily water intake just by habit stacking it with brushing my teeth. I've done this for nearly a decade now and, by habit stacking, I never forget it.

An example of habit stacking: placing a bottle of water next to my toothbrush, so I can increase my daily water intake.

Another way to stack your habits is to think about what you do when you get into your car. What can you add to your routine, something to do before you start the engine? Maybe it's taking five deep breaths. This is a quick and simple meditation exercise. Take five deep, calming breaths and get clear on your primary goal for the day.

Think through your most important habits you want to embed to figure out how you can stack them so that you don't forget. Which new habit and old habit could you pair up? Maybe you want to pair up a habit you want to develop to go with eating your meals, such as discussing as a family what you're grateful for over dinner? Or maybe you want to pair up getting clear on your top priority for the day with your morning shower? Or spend five minutes stretching while watching the news headlines or making your morning coffee? The key is to think through your habits that you do automatically and the ones you want to add to your routine and integrate. This is a practical way to change your behavior consistently over time.

Micro-habits

Micro-habits is another great concept that comes from *Atomic Habits* and is also spoken about widely by Arianna Huffington and her amazing team at Thrive Global. It's about starting off small to create consistency. It's not about making grandiose statements like many people do with a New Year's resolution where, on the first day of January, they say, "I'm going to go to the gym for an hour every single day!" It's not about starting new big habits. It's about changing your behavior over time using small habits, "micro-habits," and integrating them into your routine a little bit at a time so that they're sustainable.

Think about starting small and building consistency. Build the habit muscle. In *Atomic Habits*, Clear gives the example of building a habit of going to the gym. He shares that you're more likely to build a sustainable habit if you start with just two minutes a day actually lifting weights. Building time into your calendar for getting to the gym, making sure you have all your gym clothes, you have your playlist or podcast ready … these are all things you need to learn to do in addition to actually lifting those weights. As humans, we often give ourselves too much credit for being able to motivate ourselves to consistently perform our new desired habits. Getting the associated habits into a new rhythm consistently until you do them without thinking about it will give you a much better shot at sticking with your desired habits over time. In other words, don't bite off more than you can chew if you want to make your habits stick.

Being someone who understands the importance of exercise and staying physically active, I've played around a lot with building habits that stick. After falling ill with pneumonia, I wanted exercise to be a bigger part of my life, no matter how intense my work or life got. But what would that look like? For me, I knew that if I wasn't prescriptive in how many times a week I wanted it to happen, then it wasn't going to happen consistently. I also realized that I wanted to do something every day that would help me improve my mind and body. Make me stronger, fitter, and healthier. After thinking about it, I realized the key to success was going to be consistency.

Nearly a decade down the track of doing some form of exercise every day, what's interesting is the amount of time I spend on it. It's typically not two hours a day. But it's a minimum of ten minutes.

When I started playing around with the idea of building this new habit, I tried exercising five times a week and for an hour each time. But I failed. Then I tried half an hour every day. There were some workdays when the day owned me. Literally. I would get the kids ready for school, then have back-to-back meetings in the office, followed by looking after the kids again at home, and then work online after the kids went to bed. I'd get to 11 p.m. and just the thought of doing anything for half an hour exhausted me. It wasn't going to happen. So, thirty minutes every single day didn't work for me either.

What worked was, I realized I could always find ten minutes. That's not much time. Even late at night when I'm exhausted from the day's activities, I can find ten minutes to do something for my health. But I had to think about what made sense in terms of the activity to do in that ten minutes of my day.

On most days, since I've been doing this habit for so many years now, it's relatively easy to find that ten minutes. On other days though, when I have too much going on and I wonder how I'll ever find my ten minutes, I focus on giving myself ten "kindness minutes" for my exercise. I focus on being kind to myself and thanking myself for still finding time to do something for me.

It's not a grandiose plan. It's just looking for ten minutes minimum every day to do something that will benefit me in the long run. I've been doing it for nearly a decade now and haven't missed a day. On days when I get smashed at work, it's 11 p.m., and I don't want to get my heart rate up before going to bed, I take a little time to meditate. I simply listen to a ten-minute guided meditation as I fall asleep. I take the time to calm myself, quiet my mind, and feel good about following through on my commitment to myself. Micro-habits add up over time.

David Asch gives a fantastic TED talk, "Why It's So Hard to Make Healthy Decisions," where he talks about why it's so hard for people to change. We all know people who've been trying to quit smoking or to lose weight for years. Asch discusses the reasons habits are hard to make stick. One of the critical elements it boils down to: future rewards. There's often a reward people get right now for not starting a new good habit. And often that reward is a bigger motivator than the future reward of success. For example, if you're completely relaxed on the sofa watching TV, the thought of getting up and going for a run so that you'll have stronger bones forty years from now is probably not a bigger motivator. That reward is too far off for most people. Yet the reward of continuing to sit watching TV is happening right now. Therefore, tying a reward to an event that is closer in time is a practical way to implement and sustain good habits.

Where possible, tie in rewards that are aligned with your good habits. That's probably not going for a run then coming home and eating a big bar of chocolate. One way to approach micro-rewards and exercise is to think about how it will make you feel in thirty minutes. If you go out for a walk and get some fresh air, will you feel good about yourself? Sometimes, that's enough.

Alternatively, after you've practiced a new habit consistently, say for two weeks, consider buying yourself a small reward. This approach moves that reward forward in time instead of waiting those forty years for the big payoff.

You might have heard the saying, "No one has ever regretted a workout." The hard part is usually getting started. How do you make it as frictionless as possible, to create those nudges, so you can practice your habit consistently? Sometimes the obstacles don't need to be big to prevent you from doing what you want to be doing.

I've had days when I didn't go for a run because my AirPods weren't charged. I love listening to music when I run. If my AirPods aren't charged, then that's been enough on some days to make me say, "Nope, I won't run today." It's important to think through ahead of time all the things that need to happen for you to practice your new habit. Think through your system and the different nudges you need to employ to keep it going. In other words, remove the obstacles and objections you might give yourself.

Another obstacle for me used to be getting ready to go for a run in winter when it was cold or raining. The reward of staying warm and dry was just too enticing for me. So I rented a treadmill with the option to buy it, which I did. That treadmill has since clocked thousands of miles. Working through, ahead of time, your own obstacles, rewards, and nudges will give you a much better chance of making your good habits stick.

Your nonnegotiables

Following my own burnout story, I realized how important that advice to "fit your own oxygen mask first" was. If you don't look after yourself, and you don't have the energy or the positive attitude to be able to physically do your work, then it makes it hard to lead yourself, let alone your team.

Looking after yourself is a really smart business decision. Making it as important as attending all your important business meetings is something I've had to learn how to do. I've had to figure out my "nonnegotiables."

Thanks to Dr. Bill Mitchell for introducing me to this concept. Your non-negotiables are the activities you do outside of work that bring you joy and give you energy. For me, that's running. I'm a (very mediocre!) long-distance runner, but I love it. I love how running makes me feel. When I'm consistent with my running, it gives me so much energy, which in turns allows me to be more productive.

For some clients of mine, it's about regularly going for a walk. For others, it's swimming or knitting. For you, it could be yoga or picking your kids up from school. Or maybe it's sitting under a tree in a park and reading a good book or going out for dinner with close friends. It's something you do for your-self that makes you feel good and gives you the energy to do everything else in your life.

By its name, your nonnegotiables are the activities that you choose to commit to week in and week out—even when your work gets super busy. What's your nonnegotiable, the activity you love doing and that gives you energy?

After identifying your nonnegotiables, the next step is to think through how many times a week you want to make it "nonnegotiable" and that's also realistic. It's not just a nice to have. It's nonnegotiable. For me, running three times a week is enough to give me the energy to get through the rest of the week. If I run four or five times, that's great. But my nonnegotiable is at least three times. However, it isn't enough to simply say, "I'm going to run three times a week."

When I first experimented with this concept many years ago, I had it in my head that I'd run three times a week. What would happen though, on a busy week (which was most of them!), was that I'd get to Saturday and realize that I hadn't run at all during the workweek. I knew it was ridiculous for me to try to force two runs into the Saturday and one into the Sunday just so I could finish the week with three runs. As you can imagine, that would not be a very good approach for consistency or preventing injuries!

I had to learn how to be consistent and not just batch my runs at the end of the week. That's when I asked myself what days usually made the best sense for me to run. I decided Wednesdays, Fridays, and Sundays, in general, were the best days for me. It isn't a hard rule, but it does give me a framework for my week. When I think about my weekly goals, I schedule my runs in on the appropriate days. I don't just hope I can get a good run in on Wednesday.

Each week, I start my week with setting my weekly goals (more on this in part 3). I look at the client meetings I have scheduled, the personal events I've got on, and where practical, I then schedule my runs in for when suits on the Wednesday, Friday, and Sunday. If I've got late-night meetings with clients in Europe on Tuesday and early meetings with clients in the US on Wednesday, I know it's unlikely that I'll get up even earlier to go for a run. So I assess if it's more realistic to run later that day or schedule my run for another day, say the Tuesday. Another option I often explore is putting my nonnegotiable run on the calendar for the middle of the day on the Wednesday. It often shocks my clients when I tell them I've just been for a run and it's 11 a.m. But if that's the best time for me to get my run in, I know I'll be so much more productive working that afternoon. It's nonnegotiable.

It comes back to the outdated concept of Monday through Friday "business hours." It's not nine to five anymore for a lot of people. If you work for a global company, it's common to have a lot of early morning or evening meetings. If that describes your situation, going for a run or bike ride during the middle of the day shouldn't make you feel guilty.

One finance executive I interviewed from Google has the philosophy to "manage your energy." In a senior global role, he would often have calls scheduled early in the morning or late at night for his time zone. Instead of seeing these meetings as additive, he would simply work out what hours during his nine to five he would choose to do things other than work, such as pick his daughter up from school. The hours he chose to work would adapt based on his global commitments and energy levels, so he could be at his most productive.

If going for a walk in the fresh air at 11 a.m. is the best way to fit your nonnegotiable in, that's OK. It's going to give you the rocket fuel you need, the energy you need, to do your best work at other hours of the day. Therefore, all hours are up for grabs when looking at doing your work and your nonnegotiables. The only caveat I'd add is if it's too close to bedtime, then you might want to find another time. It doesn't help your sleep to exercise too close to bedtime. If that's the only time I have left during a day, then I typically reschedule my run for another day.

Another thing to think through is the practical aspects of your work schedule. Are there other barriers that will prevent me from getting my run in?

For instance, if I'm going to be at a client's office for a meeting, is it realistic for me to book in a run immediately after that? Maybe I could take my workout clothes with me so I can fit that in. I think through the logistics ahead of time, because those little details can easily knock me off my schedule and deter me from getting my run in.

Some of my clients choose to get their nonnegotiables in first thing in the morning, so they're out of the way. Then they can move on to business. It's up to you to figure out your way. As one executive at Microsoft says, "*You do you.*" As long as your outcomes are there, give yourself the permission to work out how to make it happen based on everything else going on in your life.

My nonnegotiable: running!

It's up to you to think about what works for your life, whether you can schedule your nonnegotiable for 6 a.m. or move it around to fit your schedule. I prefer first thing in the morning, but if other things in my life are happening then, such as meetings with my US clients, my nonnegotiable can move to a later time slot, as long as it happens in that week. I encourage you to "test and learn" to find what works for you. Through discussing nonnegotiables with numerous leadership teams, I've learned that once clients have defined their nonnegotiables, the key reasons they give for not following through on them is that they simply forget. They want to do them. But work and life just got in the way.

Scheduling your nonnegotiables in your work calendar, just like you would an important business meeting, will significantly increase your chances of following through. A simple nudge to give you the best chance of making it happen.

Many clients have also found that doing it at the start of the day (if it's not a time-specific activity, such as picking up your child from school) means that distractions are limited. It's less likely that something is going to derail you and prevent you from doing your nonnegotiables. Scheduling it after work, many clients find too many excuses and other priorities can get in the way.

Coming up with your own nonnegotiables is a fun exercise. I encourage teams to take it one step further. Have this discussion with your team, as a team. One executive at Microsoft stated when discussing how she worked and what was important to her, "*Make the implicit explicit.*" For years when I worked in corporate, I would have this discussion with my teams and we would share with each other what our nonnegotiables were. We had an app where we stored them so that, as a team, we could all clearly see what was important to each other. And we'd ask each other regularly in team meetings, "What do we need to do to respect each other's nonnegotiables?"

For example, a team member of mine loved badminton. He'd play in a badminton competition every Tuesday at 4 p.m. Previously, he would feel guilty doing this, knowing that it was during Monday through Friday 9 a.m. to 5 p.m. "business hours." He was a superstar on the team, so the fact that he wasn't at his desk from 3:30 p.m. onward on a Tuesday wasn't going to have much of an impact on his performance. We all knew not to book a meeting with him on Tuesdays after 3:30 p.m. Having that conversation as a team meant he didn't feel guilty or feel he had to sneak off to play his badminton game, given he would consistently deliver outstanding commitments week in and week out.

Often, when I facilitate this conversation with leadership teams in my group coaching programs, the leaders say, "Wow! That's so freeing."

Yes, it is.

Permission to look after yourself

If you choose to go for a walk or drop your kids off at school, you don't have to sneak in or out. People know you will be leaving early or starting work late on certain days. That's fine and simply becomes your norm. When I work with leadership teams, two words constantly come up as the leaders start grappling with switching to an "outcomes over hours in the office" mindset.

The first word is "unlearn." Many seasoned leaders learned that you needed to be in the office and working eighty-hour weeks to have a successful career and get promoted. Prioritizing your nonnegotiables, and empowering your team to as well, means "unlearning" the strategies that got you to where you are today. The second word I consistently hear leaders use, especially below the C-suite level, is "permission." Leaders don't want their bosses to think they're slacking off or aren't committed if they choose to go for a bike ride or attend their child's school assembly during "business hours." Having the nonnegotiable discussion as a team gives people permission to be transparent around what's important to them and frees them up to do their best work. Share your nonnegotiables with your team and talk about them regularly.

One other thing this does is it builds a connection with your team so that you know what's important to each other. You can also help keep each other accountable. My team would often ask me, "How are you doing with your runs this week?" If I wasn't sure if I could fit one in the next day or two, they'd remind me, "This is important. It's your nonnegotiable." Then they'd offer to cover for me in a meeting if needed or they'd remind me to figure out how I could get my runs in that week. We cared for each other's nonnegotiables.

A light bulb went off for me when I realized my nonnegotiable, my three runs, added up to only three hours a week. We all have 168 hours in a week. One of the reasons people don't exercise or do what's important to them is that they say they don't have time. But I realized that three hours out of 168 each week was not a big ask for me to do something that improves my health and makes me feel good.

It comes back to that outcomes mindset. In order for me to do my job well, this is mandatory for me. It's not about the hours in the office. It's about the outcomes produced by your hours, whenever and wherever you work them. It's about the value you deliver to your team, your customers, and your organization. As long as you collaborate effectively with the people you need to collaborate with, when and where you work is not the important factor. As one executive at Cisco told me, "It's not where you work but what you do that matters." It sets you free from the unnecessary burdens and obligations of being in an office every day.

When I need to schedule my runs for the middle of the day, I've been known to then sit down and have a client call still in my running gear (luckily, they can't smell me through the screen!). Many of them say something like, "That's great! I've never considered that I could do something like that in the middle of the day." No client has ever hinted at anything less than fascination or admiration that this is possible to do.

Another way my husband, James, and I give ourselves permission to look after ourselves is through taking three-month sabbaticals every five years. This idea comes from Tim Ferriss in his outstanding book *The 4-Hour Work Week: Escape the 9–5, Live Anywhere and Join the New Rich*. I have gifted this book to more people than any other book—for me, it planted the seed that corporate life could look very different, where employees have the freedom to choose when and where they work. Our sabbaticals have taken us to the wine regions of France, snorkeling with thousands of salmon swimming upstream in Canada, volunteering in a sloth sanctuary in Costa Rica, hiking the canyons in the United States, and even renewing our wedding vows in Las Vegas with our son Angus as our best man and our daughter Eliza walking me down the aisle as our maid of honor. Most of my happiest memories come from our sabbatical experiences. When I share these stories with other corporate leaders, the most common reaction I get is "That sounds amazing ... but I could never do that!" However, there are those who contact me down the track with such pride and excitement to share their own sabbatical experiences. Instead of thinking it's not possible, they work through how to make it happen—and I'm yet to meet someone who has regretted doing it. We're currently planning our fifth sabbatical—if you're curious to understand how you can make it happen (it's possible!), read my LinkedIn articles for details.[11]

Admittedly, I work with progressive leaders in large corporations who believe in the outcomes mindset. However, the more leaders who learn these new ways of working and embrace this as "the way we do things around here," then the greater our collective opportunity to positively transform corporate culture globally for the better.

Looking after your health is a smart business decision in addition to making you feel happier and healthier. You don't know what's possible until you give it some conscious thought. Then you realize that no one really cares at what time you run.

Keeping yourself accountable

You may have heard people say, "It takes twenty-one days to make a habit stick." In 2009, Phillippa Lilly, a health psychology researcher, performed a twelve-week study with ninety-six people and discovered that the range of new habit-forming behavior varied from 18 to 254 days depending on the individual. The average was 66 days.

A friend of mine, a chief risk officer living in Florida, inspired me. She has three kids and runs half marathons regularly. She's always got a lot on her plate. But she told me about this program she'd completed called 75 Hard. She said it was the hardest but most rewarding thing she'd ever done. I was curious about it, so I looked it up.

The idea is, for seventy-five days, you implement extreme habits to kickstart a healthy lifestyle. Two forty-five-minute exercise workouts a day, where one of them must be outside. Read ten pages of nonfiction each day. Consume

---

11 - "Sabbaticals Aren't Just for University Professors," Tina Paterson, LinkedIn 2018: https://www.linkedin.com/pulse/sabbaticals-arent-just-university-professors-tina-paterson/.

no alcohol, eat no "cheat" meals, and establish your own healthy eating plan based on your health preferences. Drink lots of water. For many, this sounds like torture. For me though, it sounded like a great challenge.

While I was keen to try it, I knew that if I tried doing it on my own, given my client schedule, my family life, and everything else, finding ninety minutes every day to do that much exercise was going to be a struggle. I also knew the data supported implementing micro-habits and starting off small—and this program was way off being a small commitment! I wanted to set myself up for success and knew the data also supported that having an "accountability buddy" would give me a much better chance of following through.

So I put out a message to about one hundred friends asking who was interested in doing the program with me. Many of them responded. Of those who responded, there were three common replies. One was a hard pass. No thanks! Some of them said, "Sounds interesting. I'm curious, but the timing's not right for me." However, twelve of them responded that they'd give it a shot. That number decreased to eight once they discovered how hard it was going to be. After seventy-five days though, there were four of us who had worked out for ninety minutes every single day for two-and-a-half months, ate healthily with no junk food and didn't drink any alcohol.

I am very clear that I would have struggled to complete the program on my own. We all have off days, where it's a struggle to do what we know we should. Having friends, or accountability buddies, can make a big difference. On the night when my friend Cath had been to a work function and returned home at 10:30 p.m. to do Pilates for forty-five minutes, she knew the rest of us were cheering her on in our WhatsApp group. When I went away for a weekend with a group of twenty friends, after we completed an eight-hour hike, everyone hung out drinking champagne together. I knew I had my support group in WhatsApp cheering me on as I sipped my soda water with fresh lime. That support group was enough to keep me going. It was also important to be able to track my progress each day and check off via an app that I had done the program requirements. It made it stick.

It's now been quite a while since finishing 75 Hard. I don't practice my new habits to the same extreme as I did then, but it's natural for me to continue drinking lots of water each day, reading, eating cleaner and exercising every day.

I had to think about which parts of the routine served me well and that I wanted to continue. Those seventy-five days of implementing healthy habits with an accountability group and checking off the list of requirements every day were things that helped make the habits stick.

Since finishing 75 Hard, I've decided that doing a minimum of 10,000 steps each day is a new nonnegotiable for me. My watch gives me the perfect nudge each day to stay on track. I see my steps so far for the day every time I look at my watch. If I don't hit 10,000 on a certain day, my watch shows my step count as blue. When I hit my 10,000-step goal, it turns orange. I don't ever want to see that blue bar, which would mean I've broken the chain of hitting 10,000 steps every day. Wanting that chain to continue provides simple gamification and motivates me to keep it going. It's a simple nudge.

Wearing a watch that tracks your steps can be a great nudge to increase your daily steps.

I have two simple systems in place to help keep me accountable to look after myself each day. My watch records my steps and shows me when I hit my daily goal. And then I have my Ōura Ring.

The Ōura Ring is one of the best investments I've made. It's a wearable ring that tracks all kinds of health data. In the morning, I check my ring data before I look at anything else on my phone. It rates how I slept the night before, what my heart rate is, my body temperature, my steps and my "readiness" for the day as a percentage. It's another nudge so that the first thing I think about each day is my health.

Remember, when you press pause, if you're feeling like Wim Hof today, it doesn't necessarily mean that you'll still feel like Wim next month. It needs to be a continual focus. Having a system in place to check it each day is a powerful motivator.

Maybe you don't want to wear a ring or a watch that tracks all that data. No problem! There are several other systems you can put in place. For example, putting a piece of paper on your wall and crossing it off each day, you complete your nonnegotiable with a bright-colored pen. Or monitor it via one of the many apps out there for tracking your goals. Or make a list of your daily routines and mark each one off as you do them, whether via an online app or pen and paper.

For me, the sustainable habits I choose look like this: minimum of ten minutes exercise today. Check. Completed 10,000 steps today. Check. Eight hours of sleep. Check. Ate five servings of vegetables. Check. Done my three nonnegotiable runs this week. Check.

Visual management is one of the best tools to hold yourself accountable, remind you of what you want to be doing, and to inspire you to keep it going.

One of the best shifts in mindset for me was when I realized that I'm human. I'm not Superwoman, a robot, or someone who is motivated 100 percent of the time. I want to bail out of practicing these habits at various stages, so error-proofing them as much as possible is critical. Many times I wanted to be on the sofa eating salt and vinegar chips instead of going for a run. Putting systems in place to help me establish the good habits I wanted to create made all the difference.

That's why I encourage you to think about the system you create as opposed to focusing on inspiring yourself. The system leads to results. Inspiration sounds good, but does it motivate you to eat your vegetables and go for a run every day? Your system gives you your best chance.

A friend of mine runs every morning, but she also loves her cozy bed. She put a system in place to motivate her to get out of bed each morning and run. She sleeps in her running gear. Yes, this might seem extreme, but she knows that this way, when she wakes up in the morning, she knows she's already made the decision to get up and go for a run. Her systems helps her know she's removed the decision-making of whether she will run.

Another friend, Cassandra Goodman, has written a great book called *Self-Fidelity: How Being True to Yourself Uplifts Your Working Life*. In her book, Cassandra shares a quote she says to herself first thing in the morning when getting up to exercise. She says, "Being half-assed is better than no-assed!" In other words, on the mornings where motivation is lacking, even if you just put in half an effort, that's better than not doing anything at all.

For me, on days when I don't feel like running, I go through a series of steps in my mind. First step, I put on my running gear (since it was in my calendar to remind me it was time for my run). Second step, I walk out the door. And I have a rule for myself. On the days when I don't feel like running, I give myself ten minutes. After ten minutes, if I still feel lousy, then I give myself permission to stop. I've had that rule in place for several years now and I can't think of a time when I've stopped after ten minutes. The hardest part is getting out the door and running the first steps. Once I do this, I remember I only have thirty or so minutes and I am done. The hardest part is usually starting.

The best nudge I've found is to put your nonnegotiables on your schedule and think about the obstacles getting between you and your yoga mat, or you and your front door.

Once you identify the obstacles, you can remove them. Give yourself a ten-minute clause. Or sleep in your running gear if that's your style.

As mentioned, I'm a fair-weather runner. Even though it's a nonnegotiable for me, I realized that I often didn't want to do it. When it's dark. Or it's raining. Or it's cold. Motivation doesn't want me to get past those obstacles. Now that I have a treadmill in the house so that I have no excuse on days when it's dark, cold, or raining. I know I have no excuses. If the weather is terrible, I run inside.

The number of hours I've been able to clock running consistently is significantly more because I was able to remove my biggest obstacle. That worked particularly well for me when my children were young. I could put them down for a nap and still go for a run, because I could jump on the treadmill and squeeze in a quick thirty-minute run. Work through your obstacles one by one and come up with a creative solution to each one. This gives you your best shot at building up your habits, one small move at a time.

The free wonder drug

Imagine I came up to you and told you this:

Amazing breakthrough! Scientists have discovered a revolutionary new treatment that makes you live longer. It enhances your memory and makes you more creative. It makes you look more attractive. It keeps you slim and lowers food cravings. It protects you from cancer and dementia. It wards off colds and the flu. It lowers your risk of heart attacks and stroke, not to mention diabetes. You'll even feel happier, less depressed, and less anxious. Are you interested?

These benefits are available to all of us and it's free. I often ask clients to guess what I'm referring to and answers I hear are "exercise," "eating well," "low stress," "spending time with the people you love" and "meditation." These are all great guesses, but the quote above comes from the book *Why We Sleep* by Matthew Walker.

Sleep is our free wonder drug.

Often, when I share this with my clients, I tell them, "If I had a pill I could give you that would achieve all this, you'd be clamoring all over each other to get to it." The interesting thing is that this wonder drug is available to everyone (although I get it's a lot harder to access for a period of time if you have a newborn baby or a child who is a bad sleeper). It's free. It's typically enjoyable (who doesn't like being warm under the covers on a cold night?), but so many people don't use it effectively.

Knowledge is great. We know we should exercise. We know we should eat our vegetables. We know we should get enough sleep. But when it comes to the benefits of sleep, we often focus on quantity and not quality as well. We focus on getting enough hours of shut-eye. But there is a miracle for most people to unlock concerning sleep. It's also about quality. Getting the right amount of hours is important, but the quality of sleep is also vital and makes good business sense too.

There have been more than seventeen thousand studies, backed up by science, on the benefits of sleep.[12] One of the best investments in time is to focus on getting enough quality sleep. Most people have heard of the magical "eight hours sleep" that we're told we should get each night. Sleep experts agree that most people need between seven and nine hours each night.[13]

Some clients say to me, "Yeah, but I can get by on six hours of sleep." Sleep experts say that the percentage of people who can function properly and make good decisions on six hours of sleep every night rounds down to ... zero percent.[14] Maybe you are one of the very few who can get by on very little sleep, but for the majority of us, it's simply not true that we can function well on this level of sleep. Several well-known business leaders say that one of the secret weapons of their success is getting enough sleep. Examples of leaders who routinely get

---

12, 13, 14 - *Why We Sleep* by Matthew Walker.

their seven or more hours of sleep include Arianna Huffington, Jeff Bezos, Bill Gates, Jack Dorsey, and Tim Cook.

I hear a lot of corporate leaders say they can function on six hours of sleep each night. In Matthew Walker's book *Why We Sleep*, he cites a study that found that when participants got six hours of sleep each night for ten days straight, they had similar cognitive reaction times as someone who has gone without sleep for twenty-four hours.

Most of us know that if we pull an all-nighter, we're not going to feel great the next day. We're probably not going to get behind the wheel of a car the next day or make significant life decisions. We know that if we go without sleep for a night, then we're probably going to be cranky. We're not going to make great decisions. We might be irrational. It's the same when you deprive yourself of a few hours of sleep for several days in a row, although you might not even realize it.

We often think losing an hour of sleep here and there doesn't matter. We think six hours is OK, but we wouldn't go all night without sleep, then go to work the next day and try to make critical business decisions. Leaders trying to live on six hours of sleep every night are living the equivalent of going all night with no sleep and then trying to work the next day. Quantity is important.

Remember also, it's about the time you sleep, not the amount of time you're in bed. If you're lying in bed scrolling through your phone, that's not time you can count toward your seven to nine hours of sleep.

I love how LeBron James looks at sleep. He's considered one of the greatest basketball players of all time, a multiple MVP winner with a harrowing schedule of games, which involve him traveling all over the United States for the majority of the year. He has several sponsorship deals that consume his time and focus. He also runs a charity, has a family, and generally has a lot going on. When he looks at his schedule, the first things he puts in his calendar are his games and travel time to those games. That's his job. But interestingly, the next thing he looks at is how he's going to get his minimum eight hours of sleep each night. He adds in wind-down time before bed as well. He schedules it into his calendar.

You might be thinking, *"But I'm not LeBron James."* You don't have to be a world-class athlete to get the benefits of sleep. It's not just for your body, although there are obvious benefits for the body, of course. It's also for your mind. James recognizes that he needs an optimal concentration level to be at his best on the basketball court. He needs to be able to make split-second decisions. He knows he needs to stay focused, and to remain cool, calm, and collected. Just like what leaders in intense corporate jobs need. He knows that sufficient sleep is the thing that allows him to do all that.

Quantity is important and deserves as much consideration of your time as your important business meetings. But quality matters too.

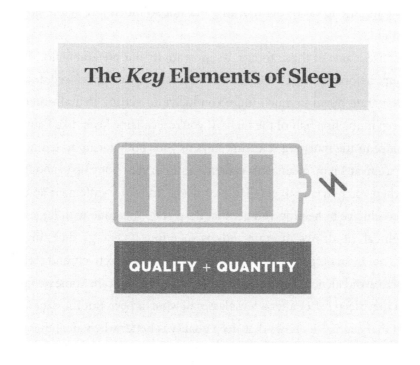

Both quality and quantity are needed to get a great night's sleep.

Not all sleep is equal. To keep it simple, experts talk about your amount of light sleep, deep sleep, and rapid-eye-movement (REM) sleep. We need as much deep sleep and REM sleep as possible. When you sleep for seven or eight hours, the quality of that sleep matters. It helps to regenerate your cells. It refreshes your mind so that you can make better decisions the next day. You can operate on an even keel and not get irritated by things that might otherwise annoy you if you're sleep-deprived.

Getting a great night of quality sleep often requires some small behavioral changes. When I discuss these small changes, these nudges, with clients, their typical response is "these changes are surprisingly doable. I just didn't realize that they made that much of a difference." But those small changes can have a cumulatively big impact. For instance, sleep experts have identified activities that are fine to do in the morning but not so much just before going to bed at night.

Exercise is one of those things. It's great to do, but preferably not in your two hours before bedtime. When it's time to sleep, feeling relaxed and with your heart rate down is much more conducive to getting that all-important deep sleep in the first half of the night. If you're a caffeine lover, like I am, have your coffee in the morning. Caffeine stays in your body for up to ten hours.[15] Having a cup at 2 p.m. means that caffeine is still in your body up to about midnight when you're trying to get that deep sleep. And since caffeine is an upper, it isn't conducive to helping you get that deep rest. The same with large meals and high-calorie drinks. If your body is spending its energy digesting your food, it's not in an optimal state to help you sleep more effectively and recharge.

Try to avoid alcohol before bed or minimize it if you can. Some people tell me that they sleep better after a few glasses of wine or beer. But the data doesn't support that claim.[16] It shows that sleep quality is better when alcohol is minimized or eliminated before bedtime.

---

15 - American Academy of Sleep Medicine at www.sleepeducation.org.

16 - *Why We Sleep* by Matthew Walker.

Where possible, have a cool room, a dark room, and a gadget-free room to sleep in. It's best between 64 and 71 degrees Fahrenheit (18 and 22 degrees Celsius).

Light can also get in the way of a good night's sleep. Close your curtains and remove or turn away any bright lights (e.g., your alarm clock) in your bedroom, so the light is out of view, where possible.

More important than darkness and the temperature is freeing your bedroom of electronic devices where practical. Being on screens just before bedtime is something that can prevent you from getting a great night's sleep. This is predominantly driven by the blue light emitted from electronic devices that delays the onset of melatonin that helps you get the good type of sleep. If you choose to be on screens just before bed, consider buying glasses that block out most of the blue light. The best solution, though, is removing electronic devices from the bedroom. If you currently use your phone as an alarm clock, take a leaf out of Simon Sinek's book: buy an alarm clock. It's a simple and inexpensive solution.

One final word on sleep. Experts agree that if you're going to stick to one great sleep habit, make it this one: Stick to a consistent sleep schedule.[17] Whatever time you go to bed at night, where possible, make it about the same every night. The same with waking up. Try to be consistent with your sleep schedule because you then teach your body to know when it's time to wake up and when it's time to start winding down and go to sleep. This is the one factor that has the most impact on sleep quality.

Mathew Portell, a school principal in the United States, is quoted as saying, "An escalated parent cannot de-escalate an escalated child." What that means is, if a child is frustrated, angry, or throwing a tantrum, then an angry parent will not be able to calm that child, because the anger feeds off itself. This quote also applies in the workplace.

---

17 - *Why We Sleep* by Matthew Walker.

I'm not saying that employees are like children! But when you look after yourself in a conscious way, it's more unlikely that you will be escalated. It is easier to be resilient and patient and therefore able to deal with any crisis at work. Things come up. Maybe someone on your team hasn't delivered something they're supposed to, or two team members aren't getting along. When you look after yourself, as their leader, you'll be calmer and better able to work through issues as they arise. You'll be more connected and able to be there for your team and whatever work and life throws your way.

When a person fits their own oxygen mask first, they usually feel happier, healthier and more in control. As Vaughn Aust says, *"Happy employees lead to happy customers which leads to more profits."*

PART 2

How to Lead Your Team

CHAPTER 4

Leading Remote Teams

"If you don't offer flexibility for your team, others will."
—Executive at ServiceNow

In writing this book, I've been privileged to interview CEOs, managing partners and C-suite executives from global companies such as Google, Microsoft, Amazon, Cisco, General Electric (GE), ServiceNow, Bupa, HSBC, Deloitte, KPMG and Accenture. One question I asked these senior leaders was: *"What are the two to three core skills that you believe corporate leaders will need to master in the coming decade in order to lead in the new normal, where teams are not in the office together every day?"* Their answers could be grouped into the following themes:

1. Trust and connection
2. Setting a clear vision and expectations
3. Collaboration and innovation
4. Communication and digital dexterity
5. Career development.

An underpinning theme that spanned across all these categories was "unlearning." That is, leaders realizing that they need to adapt in order to succeed in the new normal.

Trust (remember, they're adults!)

When you're a leader hiring other people to join your team, you spend a lot of time interviewing them, performing background checks, evaluating their technical expertise and experience to see if it matches the role you're hiring for. You're also ensuring that they're a good fit for your company and team culture. There's a lot of assessment about an individual. I've found it strange that, once the person is hired, so many leaders then think they need to look over that person's shoulder all the time to see if they're working hard.

As one HR executive put it, *"These people are grown-ups. They buy houses. They are responsible for raising kids. They look after their parents. Why would I check on them when they're working?"*

A much more effective approach is to invest the right amount of time hiring the right people, or if you're inheriting a team, getting to know them, their strengths, their development opportunities, understanding what makes them tick, and their motivational triggers.

Once you've got a good understanding of all that, why would you then treat them like a child? Why would you need to constantly know what they're working on each minute of the day?

Nearly twenty years ago, I flipped my hiring process and leadership style on its head. I decided it's better to start from a position of trust than to force employees to prove themselves. When I'd hire someone, it was because I believed they were a great fit for my team in addition to having the necessary technical capabilities. When inheriting a team, I would take the time to assess if they were a good fit for the team. I learned this philosophy, of starting all relationships from a position of trust, when I worked for an amazing leader in the United States.

It was near the beginning of my career. I'd come from a human resources (HR) background and had joined a department of three hundred people, most of whom were finance experts, operating as internal consultants for one of the largest and most successful global companies in the world. Every four months, our group of three hundred high-performers would be split into teams of two to twenty people and shipped off to one of the company's locations around the world to solve a big problem at the request of the CEO or CFO. And that problem would have to be solved in four months, in time for the three hundred of us to regroup, be reshuffled, and sent off again to another company location in another part of the world in a new team.

I felt way out of my depth and was trying to prove myself. As a young HR person—they referred to me as "the blonde HR girl from Australia"—I kept trying to prove that I could handle the assignments. You could see it in every meeting I attended and every email I sent out. My self-confidence was low; I kept doubting my work and was constantly trying to prove that I was worthy of being part of this talented group of three hundred "A players," even though I knew my financial skills were well below most of my peers with their finance degrees.

On my fourth assignment, I was assigned my new leader called Kaivan, who everyone raved about. On day one of our assignment, Kaivan called me into his office for a meeting. He said to me, "I'm so pleased to have you on my team, Tina."

I was shocked. All I could think about was how inexperienced I was at finance. I was way behind everyone else on the team in terms of finance knowledge. I was still learning. That wasn't what Kaivan focused on.

"I've heard that you're brilliant at stakeholder management and the best when it comes to being a team player," he said. "I can't wait for you to teach what you know to everyone else on our team."

Kaivan started from a position of trust. He looked at my strengths and how they could benefit our team and organization. I have never worked so hard to do my best work as I did while working for him. And not surprisingly, I produced some of my best outcomes under Kaivan's leadership. My work on that assignment led to me being recognized by the company's global CFO. I'm absolutely convinced that the results I achieved for the company on that assignment would not have happened if it were not for Kaivan believing in me and putting his trust in me from the beginning. I can tell you, he did not sit next to me every day to ensure that I was working. He simply believed that if you have the right people on your team and you trust them, then they will shine. And because of his belief in me, I was able to rise to the occasion.

Start from a position of trust and give your team members the benefit of the doubt. If they don't live up to your expectations, then you can have the conversation about expectations and performance.

I took that lesson that I learned from Kaivan on to every team that I've led since then. I've lost count of the number of people who have worked for me who have said something like, "I always tried to do my best work for you because I didn't want to let you down. You trusted me and I didn't want to take that trust for granted."

What does this have to do with leading effective remote teams? Everything. Trust is the foundation of successful remote teams. Trust your team members will choose to do the right thing, even when you're not around to see it. Every executive I interviewed for this book mentioned trust as a foundational element for building effective remote teams.

For the one or two people who might have taken advantage of my trust over the course of my career versus the hundreds who didn't, the benefits far outweigh the costs. I knew it was the way I wanted to lead. I also quickly realized that it led to higher-performing teams. Start from a position of trust, look at each individual's strengths, and work out how they can benefit your broader team. Unfortunately, there might be a handful of people who don't live up to those expectations and go down the performance management path. But I've found that they are very few and far between. Most people will rise to your expectations.

This view of putting trust in your people was backed up by several executives. As one executive from KPMG told me, *"You need to put your trust in people up-front. I've worked at KPMG for thirty-two years. Over this time I've led thousands of people. I could count on one hand those who betrayed this trust. Most people want to do a great job and are motivated and ambitious."*

I've loved giving my teams the freedom and flexibility to work from where and when they wanted, but I also saw that it made good business sense. Employee engagement went up. We achieved our team goals. I led in this way pre-pandemic, when the norm was for leaders to expect their people to work in the office and during business hours (and beyond) all the time.

In terms of voluntary turnover rate, my team's was always incredibly low. The reason was simple. My team would constantly tell me they did their best work when they were empowered to work it in around their lives. They were empowered to choose when in-person in the office made sense and when it wasn't the deciding factor. When I made the switch, I knew I was onto a winner.

This is the way people want to work. Unfortunately, it's taken a global pandemic to force employees at many large organizations to be able to work from home or remotely. According to one Harvard study (and many other studies have shown similar results), more than 80 percent of employees either don't want to go back to the office at all or would prefer a hybrid schedule, where some days they work in the office and other days they work from elsewhere, be it home, a café or somewhere else entirely. About a quarter of employees want to work full-time from home or somewhere else outside the office entirely, while around 60 percent want to work in a hybrid environment.[18]

The data shows what my gut was telling me all those years ago. Employees want the choice. And if you give them the choice, they'll pay you back many times over.

Now that most corporate employees have had a taste of working from home, it's overwhelming how many employees want to continue working remotely. According to one study by Slack, only 12 percent of employees want to be in the office full-time.[19] Some large global companies have told me that their specific

18 - "Survey Finds New Lifestyle Preferences Drive New Era for Workplace," Michele Reynolds, *Harvard Gazette.*

19 - https://slack.com/blog/collaboration/workplace-transformation-in-the-wake-of-covid-19.

company data shows that percentage being closer to 2 or 3 percent. The people who want to be in the office full-time are usually the leaders—senior managers and executives at high levels. Not surprisingly, more managers show a preference to be back in the office full-time than other employees.

There's a war going on for talent, as there often is. If you're a leader asking people to come back to the office full-time, you're going to lose the war for talent. Great employees have options of where they work and have overwhelmingly expressed their preference for having more flexibility in when and where they do their work.

What comes from this new way of working is freedom. Employees appreciate the freedom to work more on their own terms, while fully understanding the importance of meeting their work deliverables. Over the years, many of my team members and now my clients have told me that they've never been on a team in the past where that approach was encouraged and fostered. But when they have been given the chance, they have thrived in it. This way of working will be considered a base expectation for many employees in the corporate world in the future. The companies who don't get this will lose the war for talent. As mentioned, great employees always have options.

For my team to know that it didn't matter to me if they had to leave work "early" to pick up their kids from school or to go to the dentist helped all of us. It gave us all the freedom to focus on our outcomes. If there was an important meeting while they were out, we would dial them in from their car, reschedule the meeting or record it for them to listen to later. Handling it that way energized the team. They knew that their life outside of work was considered important. Many leaders still lead from the mentality that work should be everything, but not only is this not healthy or inspiring, it also doesn't necessarily lead to better business outcomes. Don't get me wrong, I love what I do. My career is very important to me, but it's only a part of what I do. It's not who I am. Through hours upon hours of discussions with my clients, I know many people who work in corporate feel this way about their jobs, but don't always express it for fear of being labeled as "not committed to their job."

Your employees have families. They have friends. They have passions and hobbies outside of work. To think that work is everything to everyone is unrealistic. It's important to encourage employees to pursue their passions, enjoy their hobbies, and focus on relationships outside of work. These are the things that can give your people the energy to do their best work.

My "outcomes over hours in the office" mantra sprung from this realization. My teams knew that I believed in this deep to my core. Every team I have led knows that I care about outcomes. The value they drive for the team, customers, and organization is vital. However, if you empower your people to deliver and hold them accountable for their outcomes, it really doesn't matter from where or when they work. Leading my teams this way has, over the years, paid me back in spades on my investment in trusting them.

Connection: creating a sense of belonging

One executive at Accenture spoke about what makes employees happy, which in turn leads to higher levels of commitment, engagement, productivity, and outcomes. He called it "The Three P's: People, Project and Place":

1. People: It's all about the people you work for and with. Previously employees would tolerate working for challenging bosses with a "command and control" approach, but not anymore. Employees want to work for leaders who set a clear vision, who lead you to the vision, and build a sense of connection and belonging along the way.

2. Project: Are you engaged by the work you're doing? Are you clear how what you do fits in with a bigger purpose and vision?

3. Place: This isn't about the company itself. It's about where you live and what you do outside of work that makes you happy, so you can bring your best self to work.

People who stay happy with their work maintain all three elements of People, Project and Place. And connection is a thread that weaves across all three.

An effective way to achieve a great connection with your team and colleagues is with check-ins. A *Harvard Business Review* article outlined that a high sense of belonging was "linked to a whopping 56% increase in job performance, a 50% drop in turnover risk, and a 75% reduction in sick days. For a 10,000-person company, this would result in annual savings of more than $52M."[20] Periodic check-ins are considered one of the best ways to develop this sense of belonging. Luckily, effective check-ins are based on your level of care for the other person and whether you're truly present with them—whether it be face-to-face or via a screen.

Consider check-ins through the lens of quadrants existing on vertical and horizontal axes. On the vertical axis, you have checking in with the whole team together versus checking in with individuals on your team one-on-one. On the horizontal axis, you have checking in about work versus checking in on their personal life outside of work. The personal includes checking in about non-work activities and it's not a "one size fits all." There are certain subtleties to think through ahead of each one-on-one, such as how comfortable each team member feels about sharing how they really feel and what's going on in their private life. Although great leaders encourage their team members to "bring their whole selves to work" (whether in the office or not), there will always be some employees who don't want to cross that line from professional to personal. The more you bring your whole self to work and share authentically, the more comfortable your team will feel in doing the same. One executive at Microsoft finishes her virtual team meetings with a "two-word check-in." Each

---

20 - *Harvard Business Review*, 2019: https://hbr.org/2019/12/the-value-of-belonging-at-work.

team member shares what two words best describe how they are feeling. When someone shares "stressed and anxious," she knows to check in with them individually when the call ends. A subtle change in language from "*How* are you feeling?" (which typically gets an autopilot response of "good" or "busy!") to "*What* are you feeling?" can often yield a more thoughtful response.

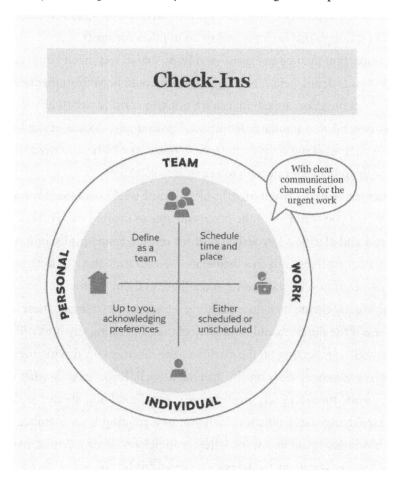

Check-ins: they're not a one size fits all.

When your team is remote, giving considered thought to how you check in with your team becomes even more important. For instance, when having a check-in with your whole team about work, regular scheduled time in diaries often works best. Have the conversation with your team to design together what is optimal, so you effectively balance increased connection and collaboration with time spent in meetings. These team check-ins could be in the form of fifteen- to thirty-minute check-ins or "stand-ups" a few times a week to see where people need help or have important information to share. These short, sharp meetings typically aren't the forum to chat about what you did on the weekend (although that is important to do in other forums!).

An important nuance an executive at Bupa shared was that it's important to reimagine your definition of "team." Your team could be your immediate team as spelled out on an organizational chart, but also consider whether your team expands beyond this standard definition. For example, does it expand to the projects you're working on or some other construct of who you need to work closely with and collaborate with to get your work done?

Other teams find a twenty-five to fifty-minute weekly or biweekly meeting works. When you're not all in the office and able to drop by each others' desks to connect and clarify, a key watchpoint for remote teams is miscommunication. Connecting frequently in a deliberate way as a team helps to mitigate this. Put team meetings on the schedule and adhere to them as often as you can.

Many of my clients then do a quarterly retrospective (more on these in part 3) to assess if the duration and frequency of their operating rhythms still make sense, as well as reflecting on the quality of the meetings for driving meaningful progress. Be super clear on the agenda, as well. Know exactly what you're going to work through each meeting. Will you be talking about roadblocks and wins? Giving status updates? Will you or a rotating team member facilitate each meeting? And as always, whether in person or via a screen, being an engaged listener is critical. Conversations shouldn't be one-sided. As an executive at Amrop Carmichael Fisher says, *"Barking orders over a video call doesn't win any affinity or loyalty."*

Susan Cain, author of *Quiet: The Power of Introverts in a World That Can't Stop Talking*, says one-third to one-half of the population are introverts. Working remotely can be like paradise for them! However, give them opportunities to reflect on what they're hearing and to ask questions. Ask them to share their views if they don't offer them up proactively. Conversely, consider your extroverts, who often crave face-to-face interactions in the office. Where practical, include in-person team meetings for fun and to share details of things going on outside of work. This gives the team the option to share as much or as little as they like and to build that sense of belonging.

When you have your team meetings, it's important not to focus on the loudest voice on the call. Many introverts enjoy working from home because they can recharge and reenergize themselves. However, some extroverts miss being in person every day with their coworkers and can inadvertently dominate meetings because they are so energized by having their colleagues around, whether in person or via a screen. In a virtual meeting, on your screens, it's a lot harder to interrupt others. Therefore, it can create a more even playing field for the introverts. However, it can also be harder to quickly scan your screen to assess who hasn't spoken for a while. As their leader, it's your job to look across your screen though and see who hasn't spoken up yet. Ask yourself, "Who might I need to encourage to speak up so that it's not just the same people on the call talking each time?"

This strategy is even more important when there are some people in the office in person and others have dialed in for a meeting. As the leader, ensuring that those dialed in are on an equal footing in terms of contributing to the conversation is critical. It's your role to create the level playing field for everyone, regardless of where they're located. A core element of this is to create a culture where the meeting happens on the call. Once a call ends, it's not a signal for those in the office to continue the conversation or make decisions. Some companies address this by ensuring that if everyone isn't in person, then those meetings are dial-ins, whether you're located in the office or not. This way, everyone is in exactly the same situation, with the same dynamics and equality. Having this candid conversation with your team, about what will work best for everyone in the team to feel connected and contributing, is well worth the time investment.

Similarly, having the explicit conversation as a team about when and how often people will be in the office is useful. I've heard numerous clients tell me that they made their hour commute into the office, only to find only three other people on their floor and then ending up on video calls all day, which they just as easily could have done from home. Many companies are using various online booking systems so employees can show their colleagues when they're planning to be in the office. At a minimum, agree as a team if you will have specific days per week to be in-person together or monthly or quarterly team days for building connection.

Individual check-ins with your team members are also vitally important, but not just regarding the work. Of course, discussing the work is a great use of both of your time, but when people have things going on in their personal lives, then it can impact their ability to get their work done. As one executive at ServiceNow said, *"If you can't meet them in a physical space, you have to meet them where they are."* You're going into their homes, with their work and life now in the same place. Having empathy as a leader is more important than ever.

It's about taking a holistic approach to leadership, caring for the whole person and not just the productive employee part of them. Taking an interest in the entire person leads to better connection, with the added bonus of also leading to better work outcomes.

It's imperative to make time for regular one-on-one check-ins, but particularly when leading remote teams. Your one-on-one meeting could be the one meeting your team members look forward to most each week. They get a chance to be with you (virtually) and discuss with you what's really going on with their work as well as outside of work, which may be impacting their ability to get things done. That's why I encourage leaders to protect their one-on-one check-ins with their team members. Schedule them on your calendar and your team members' calendars for the next six months and don't cancel them unless you or they are on leave. One-on-ones may seem like a small thing to you, but they are often a big deal to members of your team.

Rescheduling one-on-ones is not ideal, but it's OK. Things do come up, but if you must cancel a one-on-one check-in, make sure it's for a good reason. If you have a team member who is particularly struggling on the work or personal front, then try to protect their meetings at all costs.

When working with clients, I find that they are often dealing with extremes in their teams. Some team members have young children or elderly parents (or both) to care for, a busy house, and a lot going on. They're overwhelmed with noise and motion. Then there's the other extreme. Team members who are living on their own in a small apartment where they feel isolated and lonely. For those team members in particular, your check-in could be the highlight of their day, week, or month. By protecting their check-in times, you connect with your team members on an emotional level.

CHAPTER 5

I Can See Clearly Now

"Clarity is kind."
—Brené Brown

Setting a clear vision and expectations

Employees want a leader who provides a clear vision. The "light on the hill" you provide to your team provides the vision, clear strategy, and measures of success. It's then up to the team to work out how they climb the hill.

The reason outcomes over hours is important is that it isn't about saying to your team, "Don't work hard. Feel free to go home, sit on the couch, and watch TV all day." Rather, it's saying, "We're going to focus on the outcomes that matter, and those things are going to be measured. Once the goalposts are clear, it's then up to you regarding how, when, and where you work to make it happen." In other words, your employees are not staying at home to goof off. They're staying home to be just as, or even more, productive than they were while in the office. The key things that matter are the things that are being measured. The things that add value to your team, your customers, and your organization, underpinned by your company's values.

One executive at Deloitte though warns against "outcome inflation." That is, when employees are out of sight that the expectations from their leaders of how long activities actually take to get done are often unrealistic. Leaders might believe a certain task can easily get done in an hour, when two to three hours is probably more realistic. Ambitious employees don't want to be seen as taking longer than their boss expects to complete their tasks, so they talk about working a "normal day," even though their working hours might have expanded considerably.

This watch-point is well summarized: "*The move to management by out-comes comes at exactly the time when we know less than ever before about how much effort our people are expending to undertake tasks. While we want to break the nexus between hours and success, we can't lose the idea of time constraints. Otherwise, we end up with a constant inflation of expectations.*"[21]

Back to Kaivan. I could tell he believed in me. He didn't care when I did my work or if he could see me sitting at my desk working. It was all about the outcomes. That was the genesis of my thinking about leadership, trust, and indirectly about remote work. But my thoughts on this were backed up by working for another great leader years later.

Michael had a big job. He led close to one thousand employees that involved customer-facing operational roles. He'd leave the office most days between 5 p.m. and 5:30 p.m. to ensure he was home in time to have dinner with his wife and young kids. This was in the days before we had smartphones with email and other apps. When he was gone for the day, he was done. But he was known throughout the organization as a brilliant leader.

Watching Michael work, I got to see a different way of leading a team. He was ruthless with his time and where he focused his energy. He refused to be sucked into the vortex of drama, noise, or things that didn't matter. However, he always made time for his team. He understood that providing clarity to the team on the department's strategy and key deliverables, combined with

---

21 - "Working Against Outcome Inflation," Robert Hillard, https://www.infodrivenbusiness.com/.

building a team of high-performing individuals who trusted each other and worked together as a team, allowed him to walk out the office door each night at a reasonable hour.

When we formed as a leadership team, Michael ensured we carved out time to build out our department's vision and strategy. It was simple to understand and remember. No fancy words or twelve bullets to try and remember. Our slogan was "raising the bar" and showed a picture of lots of chocolate bars, with one that was a bit higher than all the others. Fifteen years down the track, I still remember it. That's the power of simplicity.

We made time to debate what operational metrics mattered, what the thresholds were for our key performance indicators (KPIs). We adopted a "traffic light system," where a metric showing as red meant it was off track and needed attention. Amber meant that we should keep an eye on it and green showed that all was within our tolerance levels. We learned to manage the KPIs by exception, only drilling in on the red or amber ones to understand the root cause and work through how to get them back on track. We'd take a similar approach with our projects and strategic initiatives. When we used convoluted language, Michael would say, "*I don't get what you mean. Simplify it for me— what are we trying to do and why does it matter?*" Yet again, we'd use our traffic light system to show which outcomes were on or off track. Transparency, clear expectations, and single-person accountability became the norm. These are outstanding leadership skills to develop, which matter even more when you're not colocated with your team every day.

We also know that if you're not sitting side by side every day, it's easy for things to get off track. The opportunities for you and your team members to be on different pages increase.

A Boston Consulting Group study found that the number one complaint that employees at global corporations had about their bosses is that they don't "communicate the team's mission clearly."[22] For your remote team, a critical

---

22 - *Ikagi: The Japanese Secret to a Long and Happy Life* by Hector Garcia and Francesc Miralles.

role you play as their leader is to provide clarity on the team's vision, strategy, expected outcomes, and measures of success. Constantly communicating your expectations and tracking and discussing progress in these areas give your team the clarity to prioritize and work on what matters most. As Jack Welch, the iconic leader of GE for twenty years, would say, "Good business leaders create a vision, articulate the vision, passionately own the vision, and relentlessly drive it to completion." When leading remotely, it's even more important to have conversations about work and expectations early on, and often, to make sure the outcomes you want are being delivered. Otherwise, you'll end up having some difficult conversations later.

Working with Michael gave me the impetus to pursue work with a different mindset. One that prioritized investing time to get clear on where we were heading and how we would transparently track and monitor our progress. This was back in the early 2000s and it was seen as a radical way to work. Taking the time to dream about what was possible. These days, not finding time for this work will leave you behind.

As one executive from Amrop Carmichael Fisher says, "*Without full knowledge of the overall content, it can be difficult to ensure that employees achieve optimum performance, are engaged and understand their purpose within this strategy.*"

Collaboration and innovation

As Vanilla Ice told us in the 1990s, we should "stop, collaborate, and listen." Along with trust, effective collaboration is a bedrock of effective remote teams.

There are times when the best way to collaborate is face-to-face in the office if you can. Being together around a whiteboard can short circuit the communication process and get a group of people working through their most important and challenging issues. It's also much easier to read people's body language and connect more deeply when you can get to catch up in person. However, as we continue to find our new normal, we know in most circumstances it won't be in the office together the majority of the time.

When you empower your team to manage their outcomes more on their terms, they will usually know when it makes sense to be in the office, sitting side by side, collaborating on a project, and when it makes sense to choose to work from somewhere else.

I prefer the term "work from anywhere" because it doesn't limit people to working from home. You're freeing up your team to work on their terms from where works best for them, as long as their deliverables are met. I do some of my best work sitting in a café with a mug of coffee in front of me. Particularly when I'm thinking and creating. I can spread my work out all over the table to work through complex problems or dream about what's possible in transforming corporate cultures over the coming decades.

Being in a different environment can also foster more creativity and innovation. Therefore, I encourage leaders to think more broadly than just "work from home." That's the default. But it's really about working from anywhere, wherever you can get your best work done, to lead to your best outcomes. One executive from HSBC, a pioneer in investment innovation, said, "*You don't always need to be with others to innovate. What you need is time and space to reflect to come up with ideas.*"

Even though I passionately believe in remote teams based on the associated benefits, I know how nice it is to be able to sit down and have a face-to-face conversation with colleagues. Like most people, I believe connection is easier when it's face-to-face rather than through a screen. Given this, thinking through how to foster collaboration more deeply and more often is a critical task for leaders of remote teams.

When I asked corporate executives their views on ensuring remote teams have some face-to-face time in the office in order to collaborate, nearly all of them said it was critically important to invest in this. As one executive at Amazon said, "*Investing in T&L [Travel and Living] expenses for a minimum of quarterly face-to-face planning, fleshing out ideas and connecting is money and time well spent."*

Being a remote team typically doesn't mean you never get to see each other face-to-face. However, what it looks like and how it benefits the team needs considered thought. One executive at Accenture predicts that a key shift will be from leaders focusing on how many days per week their employees work in the same office to focusing instead on planning events to get together in the office. These might be one- to two-day planning days that are organized six weeks out, so all team members have enough time to organize their schedules to make it in person. The in-person time focuses on reconnecting on the team vision, presenting the work delivered, celebrating successes and having dinner together to bond as a team. These days could be monthly, quarterly, or every six months. Just because your team is remote most of the time doesn't mean you can't meet face-to-face occasionally. Have the conversation as a team and work through the right rhythm for your team.

When you do have face-to-face team meetings, use them wisely since they might not be as frequent as you hope. You don't have to talk about tactical work every time you're in the office together. I'd actually suggest that's a suboptimal use of your face-to-face time. Of most importance is building the team trust, connection, and goal clarity across the team. This includes ensuring you're on the same page about where you're heading and how you're tracking. In the long run, these higher-order things matter more than the tactical work-related discussions.

Pick a pace that allows your team to meet in the office regularly enough that they feel connected. When meeting face-to-face, also place a strong emphasis on arranging connections with key people throughout the organization. Put some thought into who you can bring in to speak at your team days, such as your team's one-over leader (your direct boss) and other senior leaders in your organization so your team can get to know them face-to-face.

Extending trust is an important first step. Focusing on collaboration is a fast follower. For the past few years, Buffer has conducted an annual study on remote work. Collaboration has been rated the second biggest challenge for employees working remotely, with the biggest challenge being employees not being able to unplug.[23] Showing the next generation of new hires what a high-performing team looks like and building that on a foundation of trust is essential.

We know that about 70 percent of communication is nonverbal.[24] Body language matters. When everyone is on screen, it can be harder to "read the room" of who agrees, who has checked out, or who is really frustrated. In team meetings, it's your job as their leader to constantly scan the screen and assess levels of engagement. When people look like they're disengaged, you can simply say, "Peter, what do you think?" Use their name at the start, not the end, so they can have a couple of seconds to think about it. This also doesn't put them on the spot if their mind has wandered off for a minute!

Communicate and recommunicate with your team that debate is healthy—it's OK to have different points of view. But also that every voice has equal standing—it's not about the loudest voice on the screen. A key expectation underpinning effective remote teams is adopting the default rule of "cameras on." If 70 percent of communication is nonverbal, you don't have a fighting chance of building connection and collaboration if you can only hear your team on calls. You may have to do a lot more than simply paraphrasing and recapping conversations to ensure clarity.

Communication: getting on the same page

One of the most practical ways I've found to get things done faster is to get on the same page with your team members, colleagues, and stakeholders.

---

23 - "The 2021 State of Remote Work," Buffer: https://buffer.com/2021-state-of-remote-work.

24 - *Work from Anywhere* by Alison Hill and Darren Hill.

For years working in corporate, I had a rule that I wasn't in the office on Fridays. It was my day to take the kids to and from school, do loads of laundry and focus on my important but not urgent work. My teams knew that if anything urgent and important came up that they could always call me on a Friday versus having to wait until the Monday.

When I was the director of projects for a large organization, the CEO, whom I worked closely with, retired. In my role, I would typically meet with him and my boss, Kain, each month to confirm the agenda for our monthly strategic projects meeting with all executives. All these meetings would happen from Monday to Thursday, since I wasn't in the office on Fridays. When our new CEO started, Kain and I met with him to confirm the agenda for the upcoming strategic projects meeting. I wanted to make a good impression and so was even more prepared than usual. The meeting went well and at the end, our new CEO, Richard, said, "*Great to understand the high level. Let's meet again on Friday to discuss this in a bit more detail.*"

I hesitated. I didn't want to say no, as I knew I *could* make it into the office on Friday to meet with Richard and I wanted to show him that I was passionate about my job and career. However, Fridays were my days to do my best thinking and allowed everything else in my week to run smoothly. My boss Kain could sense my hesitation and immediately jumped in, "*Richard, Tina doesn't work on Fridays.*" Short, sharp and sweet.

Without missing a beat, Richard said in a typical Australian way, "*No worries!*" and called out to his executive assistant, "*Alicia, can you please make sure these strategic projects meetings aren't scheduled on Fridays throughout the year.*" I was gobsmacked. Here was the CEO flexing his diary just so that I could continue to maintain my boundaries and have Fridays out of the office. In that micro-moment, my levels of trust and connection with both Kain and Richard skyrocketed, as did my commitment to my job. I immediately knew I would go above and beyond to do my best work for both of them. Richard would not have given his micro-decision another thought. For me though, it became a foundation of my commitment to the company. I wanted to do my part so that Richard, Kain, and our organization could all succeed. In my books, they'd earned it. By "*making the implicit explicit*," they allowed me to continue to work in my most effective way without feeling guilty about it.

A completely different way to ensure you're all on the same page is to use the Agile term "minimum viable product." For sports fans, this is the other MVP! It's typically a messy first iteration—of a new product, a strategy, a progress update, whatever—so everyone can see it and get on the same page. It's much easier to look at a physical object and discuss it with others than to talk in conceptual terms. This also helps you to work through together whether it is really something you want to spend your time, focus, and resources on.

For example, it comes in handy when putting together presentations. In the business world, for most of my clients, creating and socializing presentations take up a lot of their time. It's an area where several hours per week are often spent.

Often, we go straight into building out beautiful presentations. We focus on making something look pretty before we ask, "What is the right content?" and "What messages am I trying to get across?" There are a series of questions that are useful to ask before you start creating any presentation. These also include, "Who exactly is my audience?" "What is important for them to know?" and "WIIFM?" (What's In It For Me?) from their perspective. Instead of diving straight into creating the perfect-looking presentation or board paper, start with creating a MVP to get the content right.

I like drawing things out by hand, but you can just as easily do it online if you want to. When people design a website, they usually don't go straight into coding and writing the page content. They first create the wire frames, which are a series of scaled-down images of what each screen will look like. It's like a storyboard. You can do the same thing when creating a presentation or a board paper. I make a sketch, a messy one, with a pen. I do it for every page of the presentation so I can focus on what the content will be. I want to first get a clear picture of the key messages and story I want to tell.

After my high-level thoughts are on paper, I share it with others as appropriate to get their feedback. Many times, since we're not in the same location, it means taking a photo of my scribbles and sending it to them. Then we jump on a video call, I share my screen, and we look at my scribbled image with these rectangles on it. Each rectangle represents a page within the presentation, and the key message I plan to convey on each page. From there, we have a focused conversation about the content of the presentation versus its prettiness.

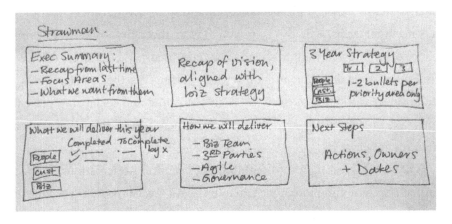

Drawing things out by hand first before making into pretty presentation format, even if ugly scribbles, can get everyone on the same page a lot faster.

The point is to make sure the story flows before we think about how it looks in PowerPoint or a similar tool. Instead of focusing on making it look pretty, the focus is on the content.

The main idea behind the MVP is to create and deliver a "shippable product." It's not perfect. As Sheryl Sandberg says, *"Done is better than perfect."* You can iterate it over time to make it better, but it's important to get something out there so you can receive customer feedback on the product. In the case of internal deliverables, it may be employee or stakeholder feedback you're looking for, or vendor feedback. Whoever the audience is, in the long run, it saves a lot of rework and back-and-forth if you can get something in their hands as soon as possible so they can give feedback on it.

For presentations, board papers and similar artifacts, the "shippable product" is the strawman, or skeleton, of the document. The more time you spend up front making it pretty before you've socialized it for feedback, the more opportunity for wasted time if you're not on the same page. If your audience says, "No, this isn't what I had in mind at all," then you've wasted that much time chasing your tail when you could have just focused on the core messages and got the same response with less time investment. So, where you can, give a "quick and dirty" version as soon as possible to get early feedback. Then, if necessary, go back to the drawing board.

Presentations take up a lot of time in most large companies. They're a key part of a leader's life. We want them to be perfect, so we spend a lot of time beautifying them. But what are they? They're a tool that organizations use to communicate key messages and to facilitate decision-making.

Organizations use presentations all the time for a variety of communications and decision-making processes. They're great tools for leaders. They're typically not used for one-on-one meetings. They're more often used during group meetings or to communicate to a group offline (e.g., for reading in your own time) and readers circulate back comments via email or a similar channel. They're often thought of as a way to get everyone onto the same page regarding a certain topic. When I speak to my clients, typically, they tell me they spend several hours a week working on presentations. Being more efficient in this area, and where possible having a conversation versus focusing on building eighty-page decks, can save leaders a lot of time. The less time spent on pages, the more time available to reinvest in adding value for your people, customers, and organization.

Recently, I worked with an executive who oversees the customer, operations, and technology components in a large global company. He combined two departments into one in his organization, and we spent a lot of time working through his long-term vision for his new department. With his leadership team, all via video calls, we talked about what the overall ambition for the department was, what the strategy was for the next three to five years and what the more tactical outcomes were to deliver over the coming year.

With this information, we developed five key pages to clearly communicate what the strategy was, why it mattered, how the team would deliver it, and what the measurements were for checking progress. These five pages were reusable. They were communicated right up to the board and executive, used in cross-functional sharing sessions, discussed with the entire department on monthly "all hands" calls and also broadly across the organization. To develop this level of clarity, it all started with a blank sheet of paper with five rectangles, each representing a different slide of the content we wanted to build. One rectangle for the department's overall ambition. Another for the three- to five-year high-level strategy. Another detailing out the one-year deliverables. Another for the ways of working. Another for next steps. You get the picture. Taking a photo of that scribbled piece of paper and sharing it with the leadership team enabled them to effectively collaborate on the content, on what was important, from nine different computer screens in nine different locations.

Digital dexterity

Another key skill for leaders is digital dexterity. Gartner describes digital dexterity as "a set of beliefs, mindsets, and behaviors that help employees deliver faster and more valuable outcomes from digital initiatives."

In the office, leaders could get away with not knowing how to use the digital channels their teams used, as they'd just drop by people's desks. As one executive from Deloitte put it, *"Twenty years ago, many leaders thought they were too important to know about technology. They focused on the business strategy and believed the CIO's team would turn the strategy into technology. Effective leaders now realize that digital skills are critical to business decisions and operating in today's world."*

Several executives spoke about leaders needing to build their "digital muscles." Innovative organizations are realizing that to get ahead of the curve, they need to upskill their leaders. Bupa has created the "Edison Data Academy," where leaders can bring their own data and put it in an "online sandpit" to learn how to analyze it, interpret it, and shift toward self-service. Deloitte has adopted language tools for working across cultures, such as live translations on calls and the ability to read live transcripts for those who prefer reading instead of listening in a foreign language.

For seasoned leaders who are not sure where to start, "reverse mentoring" can be highly effective. This involves finding a digital native or an expert in all things digital and asking them to mentor you on how to embrace the digital platforms and tools that your organization uses. In return, you can share with them your experience and expertise in business and leadership.

When a team is not constantly in the same location, effective leaders are the ones who connect and comment in the online team channels to drive that trust, connection, collaboration, and communication. What's effective in communicating clear goals and tracking progress? Digital communication is critically important for this, especially when it comes to delegating so that your team is clear on what is required of them. Keep an eye on technology trends that continue to enhance building trust, connection, collaboration, and communication across the team.

Communicating via your screen

Often on video calls, people feel the need to multitask. They check their phones and do other things when someone else is presenting or they've lost interest. Yet only 2 percent of us can effectively multitask.[25] That means it is even more important to have engaging conversations that involve participants on the call as much as you can when working remotely, because people check out sooner.

---

25 - *Think Like A Monk: Train Your Mind for Peace and Purpose Every Day* by Jay Shetty.

They feel like they can check their phone more often because no one's watching them as they hold their phone just out of sight below the camera level on their computer. So, just reading a presentation on a screen or talking at your team for thirty minutes is not going to cut it these days.

For this reason, it's important for remote teams to build their online communication skills, which starts with knowing your audience and your key messages. Consider also how you can involve and engage others on the call to make it feel more like a conversation. Where you can use storytelling to make it more interesting. People remember stories more than bland information or hard data. Rather than just telling them what you want them to know, think through how you can use stories to bring your key messages to life. If you are going to enter it into PowerPoint or a similar presentation tool, put it into wire frames first so you're clear on your messages before making them look pretty.

I learned to do this the hard way. When I started my business and all my clients were remote, I had presentations on multiple topics such as "how to work smarter" and "how to look after yourself." I thought I needed to tell them everything. I wanted to share with them every single practical tip I had. I'd have these two-and-a-half-hour to three-hour workshops where I was doing all the talking. I was just giving information to my audience. It was great information, but it wasn't very engaging. I figured out pretty quickly that this wasn't going to be effective at turning the information into meangingful action because people didn't just want to sit there looking at their screen for three hours listening to me talk.

When it comes to remote meetings, the more you can ask people's opinions, or get them to connect with each other and discuss topics, the better. The more one-way communication you have, the less likely you're going to engage your audience. The data also shows that meeting participants' engagement levels start dropping between thirty to forty minutes into online meetings, so choose your length of meeting times wisely.[26]

26 - "Our Brains Need Breaks From Virtual Meetings," Bruce Rogers, *Forbes* article, 2020.

Now, when I coach my clients, I focus on fewer strategies with them but go deeper into group discussions. It is much more engaging for leaders on the call when they can be involved and share their opinions as opposed to it being a one-way street. People don't sit through lectures via a screen very well.

Employees appreciate different kinds of communications and interactions. Some of my interactions are presentations, but I typically limit these to when I have over a hundred people on the call. Usually those presentations are forty-five to sixty minutes and don't go over ninety minutes. More than that, people tend to tune out. However, there are ways of turning those presentations into more engaging sessions. One way is to have a moderator on the call so people can submit questions via an online tool. Then it becomes like a large group chat. We usually stop every twenty minutes or so and discuss questions the audience has. It's a one-way presentation peppered with question-and-answer periods.

Another way to make virtual presentations more engaging is by conducting online polls. It may be an anonymous poll so people don't feel like they are disclosing too much of themselves. In the "press pause" part of my presentations, I regularly poll people and ask them, "Do you relate best to Wim Hof, a synchronized swimmer, or a passenger on the *Titanic*?" Polls increase engagement.

During my group coaching programs, my communications approach is to ask people to share how they're going implementing a key strategy we're focused on. I give them some time to reflect, then open the floor for discussion. One thing I've found important is knowing that some people don't proactively contribute. This happens whether you're face-to-face or remote, but when everyone is online, setting the general rule that everyone should have their cameras on increases overall engagement. It's very hard to build trust and connection when you can't see your colleagues, especially if you're the one doing a lot of the talking.

There are times when it makes sense for people to switch their cameras off; for example, they're driving, using the time as a walking meeting, they have a sick child with them, or their Wi-Fi isn't working properly. It's important to be flexible and accommodating where appropriate, but cameras on is an effective ground rule. If this isn't part of your current ways of working, have the conversation with your team about setting expectations around cameras on. Listen to their views and come up with team norms around video call etiquette.

When I have small group discussions, before the call, I write down the names of everyone on the call and make sure that I'm inviting participants to speak in rotation so that every voice is heard and everyone knows their opinions matter. I invite everyone to contribute at different times throughout the call. Doing this ensures it's not the same people talking every time. A louder or more frequent voice does not necessarily mean that what they say is more important or valid. Another benefit to this communications approach is that everyone on the call knows they're expected to contribute. They know they're expected to share their ideas and views and not just sit there and listen.

CHAPTER 6

Out of Sight, Out of Mind?

"I don't like it, but I fear that without considered and deliberate action and initiatives, we might inadvertently create two classes of high-performers: those who still get picked for the special projects because they choose to spend more days working in the office and those who are just as good, but because they choose to work more from home they don't get picked, because no senior leader except their direct boss knows who they are."
—Corporate executive

The unfair advantage?

Many executives I interviewed spoke candidly about a significant watchpoint they envisioned with remote teams. Many shared that some of their own best career opportunities, such as being chosen to work on a special project or even getting promoted, came about because of the relationships they had built with senior leaders face-to-face over their time in the office.

The quote above is a pretty blunt prediction, but without that "considered and deliberate action" from you as their leader, it's a very plausible prediction.

When I worked at GE, we had an amazing career development model that we referred to a lot called the PIE model. The *P* stands for performance, the *I* stands for image and the *E* stands for exposure. They're all important elements for building your career.

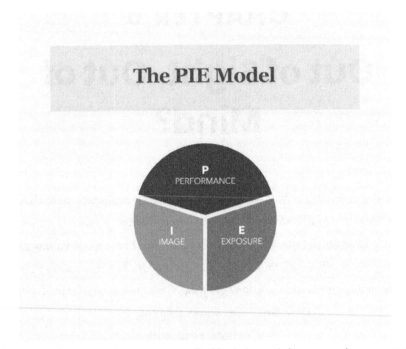

Performance, image, and exposure are all critical elements for progressing your career.

Unsurprisingly, performance is considered important to advance your career. Careers are developed on performance. However, it is only one piece of the pie. A core philosophy of the PIE model is that no one is promoted solely on that one piece of the pie. Another piece of the pie is image. This component is the one that people often don't talk about. GE leaders did a brilliant job of highlighting to employees that how they conduct themselves at work is important. Professionalism, confidence, and courage to try new things are all important aspects of your image that contribute to building your career.

When it comes to leading remote teams, the one piece of the pie that leaders need to intentionally think about is exposure. It's important for all team members, but particularly for your emerging talent, your external hires, and those who are in the early stages of their careers. It's important that senior leaders know who these people are and get to know the best talent in the organization, so that when the promotions, special projects, development programs, or other career opportunities come up, your best talent has the opportunity to be selected. Not just those who choose to work an extra day or two from the office each week.

From a learning standpoint, some of my best education came from being around the CEO or other members of the C-suite, especially when I was in the early stages of my career. I'd see how they conducted themselves in meetings and observe them from a distance while they were chatting with their team members. I worked out the type of leader I wanted to be, based on who I decided were my role models through observing them in the office. Those kinds of observations are harder to make when you're working remotely. Therefore, extra effort needs to be made to ensure that you're giving your team, particularly emerging talent, external hires, and those in the early stages of their careers, similar exposure opportunities to those you might have had years ago.

As an executive from ServiceNow commented, "*You need to create serendipity in a virtual world.*" Whether that is deliberately connecting people in online break-out rooms or getting your star performers to present in an 'all hands' virtual call just before the CFO speaks as your guest speaker, you play a major role in "creating the serendipity."

As some of your team will probably spend more time working in the office while others spend more time working from outside the office, it's your job as the leader of all of them to create these exposure opportunities in a fair way for all. Be deliberate about creating networking opportunities for your team. Consider external speakers. That could be external to your organization or external to your department. Invite a finance leader for a "lunch and learn" session to talk through the organization's profit and loss (P&L) statement and balance sheet with your team. Invite the head of operations to share what customers like and don't like about your company's products and services. Or the head of sales to share the company's growth strategy. Or senior leaders to share their career highlights, lowlights, and insights on what has most contributed to their career success to date. It's important to pass on to the next generation of leaders some of the knowledge and experience that has been building in the organization for many years. As you're in a position more senior to your team, you're in the perfect position to create these exposure opportunities for them.

Where possible, also think about networking with other departments in your organization. Where are there cross-functional opportunities for your team? If there's a project coming up, who could learn most from getting broader exposure to the business? When people work on a team with other people from marketing, HR, operations, IT, and finance, they learn broader business skills from others in those meetings through osmosis. Even through a screen. They get to see how people think differently about the work and the organization. It's a great way to build capability in emerging talent. Give your team a chance to learn about different departments and leaders. Encourage them to ask questions. Help your team get those general business skills that are more challenging to develop when not in the office every day.

One executive at Google takes advantage of the company policy where employees can work for up to four weeks per year from any other office. Although he usually works out of the Paris office, each year he spends nearly two months in his hometown of Mexico City with his family: four weeks on vacation and four weeks working from the Mexico City office. As he says, this arrangement benefits Google as well as him. He builds strong networks and relationships with colleagues in this region, which facilitates best practice sharing throughout the rest of the year for him and his team.

Exposure and networking are very important and your remote team relies heavily on you to help make it happen. It's important for your people to be exposed to the senior leaders at your organization. Numerous times, I've seen people get tapped on the shoulder for a different role or for a special project and it was usually because they had met someone in a senior position who thought they had potential.

It's important to create those opportunities for your remote team members even if they're not often in the office with key decision-makers every day. In the office, employees can bump into senior leaders relatively easily, but it's more difficult to casually interact with senior leaders while working from home. That's why it's important for leaders to create exposure opportunities for their emerging talent so they can show their true worth to key influencers.

As I said earlier, hosting lunch and learns with experienced leaders from throughout the organization is a great option. If adopting this strategy, encourage your team to ask questions of the speakers. Twenty years ago, when I was fortunate to be a part of that global group of three hundred high achievers, every four months, we'd get together for a conference where we'd have the most amazing speakers join us. CEOs, CFOs, and industry experts would come and talk to us. Our department head would constantly say to us, "Be curious. Ask a question."

What I realized many years later was that asking the speakers questions were micro-opportunities for exposure. When you ask a brilliant question, the person giving the presentation may want to know who the person is asking it. Other leaders and peers are listening, too. That's a moment to shine, an opportunity to impress, in addition to hearing answers to the questions you want to know more about.

I experienced and benefitted first-hand from this type of exposure near the start of my career. I was in the human resources leadership program at one of the largest companies in the world. There were about ten of us on a graduate program in Australia and every month, we'd meet with a different C-suite member to learn about their career and hear their advice. About four months into my career, our "lunch and learn" was with the CEO for Australia and New Zealand. We were all really excited for this exposure opportunity.

Our CEO, David, shared nugget after nugget of career advice with us and we all furiously took notes. He then started sharing his perspectives on what it took to be a great leader. He shared his views on when to empower versus involve your teams when you're the leader. I thought about what he'd said and realized that I had a different view. As a young twenty-three-year-old, only four months into my career, I shared my differing views with David, the seasoned and distinguished CEO. I looked around the room and saw the looks of horror on my fellow graduates' faces. The penny then dropped that this was probably a career-limiting move to disagree with the CEO about his definition of great leadership!

After the meeting, my peers asked me why on earth I thought it was a good idea to disagree with our ultimate boss. A few hours later, Ian, our HR director, called me into his office. I felt sick. I was waiting to hear the words, "You shouldn't have spoken up. You shouldn't have disagreed with the CEO." Instead, Ian said, "David was impressed that you had the courage to discuss an alternate view with him. He wants you to do your next six-month graduate program rotation working directly for him." This opportunity to work directly for David accelerated my learning and career exponentially. I am very clear though, that I would not have had that opportunity if it weren't for speaking up and getting that exposure in the first place.

Think about exposure opportunities also for your new hires. It's nerve-racking to start at a new organization or with a new team. Doing it remotely adds another level of challenge. It's important to be deliberate about working through how you set them up for success in addition to all the typical things you do with other team members, such as one-on-one meetings.

It might make sense to have a few more one-on-one meetings with new hires during the first couple of months. Remember, they can't just walk into the finance department and say, "Who should I speak with about this particular question I have?" When everything and everyone is new to them, they need someone to translate for them, and to help them learn "who's who in the zoo." Setting new hires up with a buddy or delegating to someone on your team to help them get settled in, can also be of big benefit.

Another way to create exposure opportunities for your remote team members is to get them to present their work to management wherever possible. Mediocre leaders take every opportunity to present to management for themselves, even when the work and presentation were done solely by a member of their team. It's not realistic for your team members to present every time, and your own exposure is also vitally important, but thinking through how to create the right exposure opportunities for your high-performing team members and their work is a huge part of their development. It also helps to motivate them, which in turn leads to better outcomes.

Feedback and coaching

Structured operating rhythms, where you can give regular coaching and feedback to your team members, are important parts of developing their careers. There will be millions of people coming into the corporate workforce over the coming decades. People new to the workforce are like blank canvases. They need guidance from you to thrive, but even more so when they don't consistently get to learn from you and their colleagues in the office.

So much on-the-job learning in the corporate world is done through osmosis. Over the decades, many junior employees have been trained in crafting their "elevator pitch." The elevator pitch was designed for the scenario when you're in the office and you bump into the company's CEO / CFO / C-suite member as you get in the elevator with them. What do you say when they ask you, "So, what do you do here at the company?" You know you have about thirty seconds to deliver a compelling answer, before they get out of the elevator.

Employees are trained to give their elevator pitch clearly and concisely within thirty seconds. That skill has previously been learned and put into practice in the office. Leaders now need to think about how their team members can acquire those skills and have the opportunity to use them when they aren't regularly bumping into executives in the elevator or face-to-face. That's where coaching and feedback from you are vital to help bridge the gap for your remote team.

Another key data point for leaders of remote teams is that only 20 percent of feedback given is planned. When in the office, a whopping 80 percent of feedback given is unplanned.[27] For instance, after a meeting in the office, when the leader and the team member are walking back to their desks, the leader might say, "Hey, I noticed in that meeting ..." Unplanned feedback on the spot. When you conclude a video call, however, it takes that little bit more effort to connect again with your team members and give them feedback. It's your duty though, as a leader, to think through how and when you deliver that unplanned feedback. Having regular one-on-ones scheduled is a great solution to give you this time for deliberate and considered feedback.

Feedback is most relevant when it's timely. Holding on to something that a team member hasn't done well and giving them the feedback in their annual performance appraisal five months later isn't going to have anywhere near the same impact as near real-time feedback. Giving your team members timely and considered feedback is one of the most effective strategies in building the capabilities of your remote team, as well as maintaining connection.

One-on-one coaching is very important. It's important for new hires into the company, people in the early stages of their careers, and seasoned employees. Situational leadership theory, developed by Ken Blanchard and Paul Hersey, is a useful model to help leaders determine the coaching style that's appropriate for each team member, depending on their development level and experience. Not everyone in your team is going to be at the same level of capability for a lot of different reasons. What you delegate to each person is going to change depending on whether they're new to the organization, their individual abilities, and their experience.

Who are the experienced people on your team who may not need as much of your time? Who are the new hires who need extra help in knowing who's who in the company and might need a quick introductory message to connect

---

27 - *Work from Anywhere* by Alison Hill and Darren Hill.

them? Who's new to the workforce and needs to be taught basic skills in how to succeed in the business world?

Effective leaders make sure their approach is based on the individual. It's not a blanket leadership approach of delegating the same type of work to everyone, because everyone isn't at the same level of capability or experience. Identify those people you need to spend more time with and reflect on what exactly they need from you. With remote teams, it's about making time for work and time for the social stuff, but also time for coaching and developing your team members. Being deliberate about having one-on-one coaching time has a huge return on investment.

Think also about what you can also do to recognize your team members. When remote, it's even more important to keep your team connected and feeling appreciated, particularly as you cannot always see the effort your team members are putting in. Some team members might need additional reassurance from you to know they are on the right track, so connect often so you can give praise when it's due and guidance when needed.

Like feedback, knowledge sharing across your team helps build your team's capabilities and expertise. This also needs to be more considered when you're not all located at desks next to one another. Think about your meetings and what happens during them. Do you need to debrief your team on conversations with your boss or peers, so your team has the right information to do their jobs or remain connected to your organization? What questions were asked? Are there any insights into other leaders' perspectives or ways of working to share? Give your team members multiple ways to learn so that it's not always by osmosis.

Bring in the experts

Ongoing professional development is another great strategy to build your team's capability. Punchy sixty- to ninety-minute virtual learning and development sessions can significantly increase learning outcomes. These days, it doesn't always have to be in a classroom together. Nearly all of my group coaching programs are online, which also reinforces the work from anywhere philosophy. I've learned that two hours is the maximum time I'll typically deliver online at a time. I've found that shorter, fifty-five-minute sessions weekly over three to six months are optimal for embedding new skills, with monthly check-ins from there.

These days, teams have access to great technology and online tools, including different platforms for video calls. You can use these tools to build your team's strategic performance plans. You can use them to build your team's personal development plans. Who are the best speakers and coaches when it comes to professional development in the areas that will make the most difference to your team? Don't just skip learning and development because it isn't face-to-face. If you need help with that, working with a coach like me can set you and your team in the right direction.

Be a "person-first" leader

The core components leaders of effective remote teams focus on are building foundations of trust, connection, and collaboration; being clear about the team's vision; and helping their employees develop their careers. This is all while giving their people the freedom to work on their own terms the majority of the time.

Team members typically need recognition and reassurance a lot more when they don't see you every day. They want you to be rock solid as their leader, and to know that you're there for them even if they have a slump and are not doing their best work for a period of time. One saying I use with my clients involves "peaks and troughs." There are times when there are significantly more priorities and deadlines than usual that coincide at the same time; then it usually dies down a bit. The same phenomenon happens for people outside of work.

You might not know what the peaks are or when they're coming. Maybe there's a sick family member, their own health issues, or they're going through a separation with their spouse. Unless you have built a strong foundation of trust and connection with your team members, they might not open up to share those things with you. Nevertheless, those are peaks that can have a significant impact on the work. Maybe you need to ease off delegating to that person for a while so they can deal with the issues outside work. If they're an amazing employee, you can give them less to focus on and then ramp it back up once the situation is better under control.

This leadership philosophy focuses on the "person first." My favorite leaders, who I did my best work for, were fully committed to developing me and my career, but also took the time to know what was going on for me outside work. Through watching how they would lead, I realized that taking a "person-first" approach was a constant in how they worked and led their teams effectively.

In my first year as a leader, I had an unfortunate situation of putting the "person-first" concept into practice. I was working overseas and was leading a team spread out across the United States and Mexico. One of my team members, Carlos, was from Mexico City and on this assignment was also based there. Carlos had a report due to me one Monday, and the report was going to move on from me to the organization's global CFO. Come Monday, I hadn't heard from Carlos. I emailed him in the morning asking for the report. Early afternoon, I got a call from him and learned that his best friend had been kidnapped there in Mexico City. The kidnappers were asking for ransom money from the family. Carlos didn't know whether his best friend was still alive. As a leader, I had a dilemma. We had this huge report due to the global CFO and the team member who was due to deliver it was, understandably, broken up over his missing friend. I realized right then that my approach needed to be *person first*.

Twenty years later, I can't tell you what that report due to the global CFO was about. But I get emotional thinking about Carlos.

Carlos needed a calm and reassuring friend at that time. He didn't need a manager.

I called up the rest of the team and said, "Drop everything. We're creating this report today for the CFO." To Carlos, I said, "Don't worry about it; the team's got it." Then, I emailed the global CFO and said, "I'm sorry, but there have been unforeseen circumstances and I will be a day late on this report. I'll have it to you by tomorrow."

The team pulled its weight and delivered the report so that Carlos could be where he needed to be—with his family and friends. Thankfully, there was a happy ending to the story. His friend was released a few days later and, after a few weeks in the hospital, made a full recovery. After that, my connection with Carlos increased dramatically. And as I write this twenty years after that awful incident, I'm so proud that Carlos is now a successful CFO himself. Knowing that many brilliant employees have a blip of time when they are not at their best, and that you and the team are there to help them get through it, is not only the right thing to do, but also can create deep and long-lasting relationships.

CHAPTER 7

"Unlearning"

"What got you here won't get you there."
—Marshall Goldsmith

This kind of transformative change calls for a mindset shift. As one executive from Accenture says about the future of work for corporate leaders, *"Not only do you have to change, you have to know you have to change. If you don't, you'll get left behind. You will pay the price."*

For decades, most corporations have operated Monday through Friday from 9 a.m. to 5 p.m. as their "business hours." For the past couple of decades, since the emergence of the Internet, those business hours have expanded to more closely resemble "around the clock," particularly in large global organizations. Employees still work their "business hours" in their own time zone, but often then add in early morning and late at night calls to cater for their colleagues' "business hours" in other time zones.

It's time for leaders working in corporate roles, particularly if they have a global component, to radically overhaul this way of thinking.

Challenging the "business hours" concept

Let's start with blowing up the idea that you should work Monday through Friday from 9 a.m. to 5 p.m. Let's rid ourselves of the idea that those have to be your team's most productive hours.

Some amazing companies around the world are trialing different work models that blow up the long-held view that working in an office from Monday to Friday from nine to five is the optimal way. One company in New Zealand, Perpetual Guardian, piloted a four-day workweek with no drop in pay. They found that productivity did not drop and their engagement scores, as well as several other business metrics, thrived. The company's founder, Andrew Barnes, discusses the benefits for employees and the company in his wonderful book *The 4 Day Week: How the Flexible Work Revolution Can Increase Productivity, Profitability and Well-Being and Create a Sustainable Future*.

Barnes's book explores other companies also challenging the notion that we should all work Monday to Friday, nine to five. When companies have the courage to implement it, there have been great results. The five-day workweek has been with us for a long time. People got used to working Monday through Friday; then the weekends crept in. Many people work on Saturdays and Sundays, too. To break up that pattern is hard because a lot of people think the more work you do, the better. But it's simply not true most of the time.

Quality over quantity delivers far superior results. Aubrey Marcus has written a fantastic book titled *Own the Day, Own Your Life*. He talks about how you can "own" your day. That is, if you don't take charge, proactively and to consciously think through what you're doing, then the day owns you. You get to the end of the day and say, "What on earth have I done today?"

Throughout the book, Marcus talks about the science and the data behind work productivity. One recommendation he makes, which is backed up by science as to its benefits and link to productivity, is to take an early afternoon nap for twenty to thirty minutes. When I speak with my clients, most of them say, "I couldn't take a nap in the middle of the day. It would make me feel too guilty." When I worked in corporate, I experimented with taking a nap in the middle of the day. I felt guilty for taking that twenty to thirty minutes off to have a nap.

I knew that scientific data supported the practice of afternoon naps. But I still struggled. Even now, while I know it's a great use of time, I only do it on days when I just don't have the same level of energy as I did in the morning. I don't do it every day, even though I know it can be a really productive tool to get my work done more effectively.

We have so many behaviors we need to unlearn. The Spanish were on to something when they invented afternoon siestas.

The reason I spend so much time talking about inputs and outputs is that a leader's key role is to drive value for their people, their customers, and their organization. That's assuming they're doing it with the right values and collaborating with the right people. To the extent that they do that, that's a sign of their commitment and abilities as an employee and a leader.

I don't believe in outputs at all costs. Delivering outputs in the right way matters. Working one hundred hours a week and answering all your emails at 11 p.m. are not the hallmarks of an effective leader. We need to talk about how we can change this mindset in the corporate world. When someone says, "I'm so busy," my mind shoots straightaway to that picture of the cavemen pushing the cart with square wheels. That's the mindset and culture we need to shift in order to lead our remote teams effectively.

Language is important too. Instead of celebrating the person who worked all weekend, celebrate the result instead. Your leadership shadow is long. People hear what you say and watch what you do. Think through whether you're rewarding your people for working crazy hours or if you're focusing on how they deliver value. It's OK to be flexible when your employees have things going on outside of work. Anticipate their energy levels.

We want our energy levels to peak between 9 a.m. and 5 p.m when it's the typical corporate workday. However, some people do their best work at 8 p.m. That's OK. Some do their best work at 6 a.m. That's fine too. We can still collaborate effectively, even if we're not working the same hours. The more you discuss this as a leader, the more impactful it will be on your team and they'll feel your permission to experiment with working differently than they have in the past. This involves unlearning the old ways of work and forming new habits and norms. Matt Mullenweg, cofounder of WordPress and founder of Automattic, is a pioneer in this field. His excellent article "Distributed Work's Five Levels of Autonomy" is well worth reading.

Leading by example is important. When I worked in corporate, I made a point to "leave loudly." When I was in the office and had to leave during typical business hours to handle something outside of work—to pick up the kids from school, for example—I'd exit loudly. I didn't do it every day, but when I did, I made sure everyone knew it.

I'd walk around the office to each team member and say, "I'm going to pick up my kids now. I'll be available in two hours if you need me."

By modeling this behavior right in front of them, they knew it was OK for them to do it too. That's much more powerful than saying, "You can work when you want." Whatever it is, whether it's competing in a badminton tournament, going to the doctor, or going for a surf, if you leave loudly, your team will know that when and where you work are not the most important factors in being a great employee. When you're not all in the office together, setting the culture around "outcomes over hours" is even more important, so employees don't feel they need to sneak off or feel guilty about an 11 a.m. dentist appointment.

After having my first child, when I returned to work, I received some great advice. A friend said to me, "Before having children, you can work whatever hours you want. Once you have kids though, you have responsibilities to pick them up from day care and drop them off. You can't outwork other people any-more by the number of hours you put in. You must be able to work efficiently and be more effective with the hours you do work." She continued. "When you leave at the end of the day, whatever time it is, walk out with your head held high and know that you've produced more than a full day's worth of value."

When you push toward a hard deadline, whatever time it is, you'll get so much more work done than someone who feels they have all the hours in the world.

My friend's advice was very wise. It's applicable for everyone, not just people with kids. Giving yourself and your team permission to focus on creating value in the most effective and efficient way so you can free up time to focus on things that matter outside work makes good business sense and leaves a leadership legacy you can be proud of.

Shift from activity to impact

Reevaluate your time. Discuss as a team where you spend your time and when you're most productive. Using the 168 hours exercise, which I will share with you in part 3, will help you to do this. What are the most value-added activities that you can bring to your life, from a work and personal standpoint?

In other words, for work: What will drive the most value for your team, your customers and your organization? And personally: What will drive the biggest impact for yourself, the people that you love, and your community?

The most productive thing you can do may be looking after yourself. It could be going for a run or speaking with a loved one. If that gives you the energy to be more productive for a few hours, then do that.

It's not just about shoving more work in or needing to be in the same room. It's about thinking about the most productive use of your time. Consider approaching this in three different categories:

1. What is the highest form of productive work, aligned with our vision, that my team can deliver?
2. What can I do to look after myself right now in terms of physical and mental health?
3. How can I connect with someone—be it a colleague, team member, stakeholder, a family member, friend or someone in my broader

community—that will deepen our relationship? And does it need to be face-to-face or will online suffice?

The main thing is to consciously choose your actions as opposed to meandering through your day and thinking as you get ready for bed, "So … what have I actually done today?" It's about consciously thinking about all your waking hours and putting them to the best use for you. Each day will be different in terms of what is most important to free up some time for and where to reinvest your time.

Your SCD ratio

Through the work lens, a strategy I discuss with clients to work out what their most productive work is, is what I call the "SCD ratio." This involves assessing their comparative time spent on strategy versus coaching and leadership versus doing. I encourage leaders to think about the ratio between where they spend their work time:

1. Strategy: How much of your time is spent on strategic work? This includes taking the time with your team to get clear on your vision, the long-term strategy, your twelve-month goals, quarterly/ monthly/ weekly planning, establishing KPIs and systems to track them, and communicating and recommunicating all this with your team and stakeholders. Everything that will drive your team toward being clear on the work that matters in the foreseeable future.

2. Coaching and leadership: How much time do you spend on coaching and leadership? The key activities here are usually building capability in your team, so you can empower them even more to take on bigger and better tasks. This includes one-on-ones, effective team meetings, "all hands" departmental calls—all tasks that help your team to be able to deliver on the team's big ambitions. Time spent partnering with key colleagues and stakeholders is in here too.

3. Doing: How much of your work time is spent in the weeds doing the lower-level work? Often, when I start working with clients, their time spent on "doing" in their SCD ratio is very high, typically at the expense of taking the time to get really clear on their strategy or coaching their team.

An effective leader of remote teams is typically high on the "S" and "C" and lower on the "D" with their SCD ratio. Hardly any leader gets away with no "D" though! But the most effective leaders will do a lot less of the tactical tasks. When work comes across their desk that makes sense to prioritize, their first question isn't "*How* will I do this work?" but "*Who* makes the most sense to do this work?" By asking this different (and better) question, they are able to consciously free up time to reinvest in more strategic work and coaching.

Coaching your remote team is your ticket out of being busy. It's the way to build and empower your team so that you can delegate more of the doing. You can then either not action certain work because it's not a priority or you can choose to delegate it. You give it to your team. The way to feel confident with this approach though is to ensure your team has the capabilities to work through on their own how they will do the work so you can delegate the higher-order issues for them to figure out and deliver the solutions, instead of spelling out a laundry list of tactical tasks for them to tick off.

This requires investing in building your team's capabilities. The goal should be to free up your time to focus more on the strategy and coaching elements.

Coaching is an example of something that is important, but typically not urgent (more on this in part 3). Your organization probably isn't going to fall apart if you coach your team members this week or next. It's easy to think, "I could do it so much faster myself." But it's about building your team members' capabilities, layer by layer. Over time, the more you coach and teach them, the more you'll be able to step out from the weeds and delegate with confidence regarding the outcomes. Chances are it won't happen though unless you spend time investing in that important-but-not-urgent work with your team.

Being OK to fully delegate and empower your team needs one critical ingredient, irrespective of their capabilities. It rarely happens unless you trust your team.

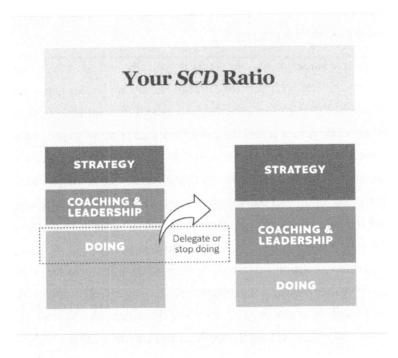

Think about the amount of time you spend on strategy, coaching & leadership, and doing.

Survival of the fittest

As mentioned, when I asked the executives I interviewed what they believe is the number one thing needed for remote teams to be effective, most said trust. My clients also consistently support this view. And I agree.

There are two approaches I've seen leaders take with trust. The first is, you make your team earn your trust. The second is, trust is given from the outset and it's yours to lose.

In the first situation, the team is constantly trying to prove that they can do the work. Significant time and effort go into proving themselves, trying to show how hard they're working. In these instances, the focus goes to the process—showing how busy/committed/hard-working the person is instead of focusing on the outcome—even if it does get done in half the expected time. In the second situation, you take the much more effective approach of just trusting your team from the outset.

Having this leadership approach is one of the best decisions I've made in my career. It's a rare person who starts a new job wanting to fail or mess it up. Most employees want to do a good job and their boss is usually the first person they really interact with in the company. Their boss acts like a bird who "imprints" on their baby birds: They set the tone for either inspiring their teams or setting a command and control leadership style with low levels of trust. The boss is the key person who will imprint on their team, and it's up to them as to whether this is in a good or a bad way.

The number of team members who've let me down, I can count them on one hand. Most of the people I've worked with have felt the trust immediately and done the work needed so they weren't letting me down. They didn't want to lose the trust, as they knew the freedoms that came with it.

Start with trust. Then, it's each individual's to lose, as opposed to theirs to earn. If you go in with that as a team principle, you can build on top of that. From there, focus on the micro-moments that can either build that trust or erode it. Look for the micro-moments to demonstrate that you're there for them through actions, and not just words.

Unlearning ways of leading that might have made you successful in the past and adapting to this leadership style that results in building effective remote teams is one of the best investments of your time and effort. It's important AND urgent to do.

PART 3

How to Achieve Extraordinary Outcomes without Burnout

CHAPTER 8

Be Clear on What Really Matters

"Starve your distractions, feed your focus."
—Daniel Goleman

T he reason corporations exist is to drive value for their customers, via their employees, and the organization, whether that be for shareholders, the community, or some other construct. Corporations don't exist with the ambition of creating lots of meetings or for emails to go back and forth from one employee to another.

Whatever your company's structure, remember the three lenses of value. Your people, your customers, and your organization.

It's not a hard-and-fast rule, but most organizations have three main constituents—employees, customers, and the organization itself (with various beneficiaries, such as shareholders or the community). It's like a three-legged stool. If you just focus on customers, then you might not be taking care of your employees. The customer will then lose in the long run. If you're not focused on customers, your financial sustainability will be in jeopardy in the long term. If you only focus on the organization, often via shareholders, then your employees and customers will eventually lose out. You need all three to be successful in the long term.

That's why it is important to continually return to your purpose at work. Why are you employed at your organization? What activities do you do that really matter and make a difference for your people, your customers, and your organization?

In part 2, How To Lead Your Team, I shared that numerous corporate executives I interviewed shared that setting a clear vision, strategy, goals, and expectations is a critical skill for leaders of effective remote teams.

There are many studies on the power of setting goals. If you're not clear where you're going, you'll just meander along with limited results. That's why one of the most important things you can do is be clear about the most effective work for you and your remote team.

Some of my most impactful work with different companies has been where we spent time defining the vision, the strategy to get there, the measures of success and how to transparently report on them on a regular basis. You've likely heard the saying, "What gets measured gets managed," by Peter Drucker.

Whatever you put under a spotlight is the activity your people will focus on. Therefore, make sure you've got clear goals to start with and are clear about what those SMART (specific, measurable, attainable, realistic, time-bound) goals are. But you must also be proactive in tracking and visibly sharing your progress toward those goals, particularly as you're not all in the same location. I've seen too many leaders to count who have created inspiring SMART goals at the start of the year, only to revisit them again for the first time six months down the track when it's their half-yearly performance review. They hope they've focussed on the right things throughout the year. And to quote that CFO I used to work with, "Hope is not a strategy."

If you're a part of an organization, you need a process or system for deciding what is of the most value. What should you and your team focus on? The problem is, typically, there isn't one process or system.

For instance, if you're the head of legal, chances are you're going to focus more on protecting your organization than making sure that everything the customer wants they get. You'll assume the head of product or head of marketing will spend more time focusing on the customer and your primary role is to keep the company safe. In other words, whether you dial up one lever (customers, employees, organization) or another is largely based on your role within the organization. That's an important nuance to grasp, particularly when you're in a role with multiple stakeholders with competing priorities.

The Ivy Lee method

It's really easy to get sidetracked at work and go into reactive mode. Frantically answering emails in the one minute you have in between back-to-back meetings. It's easy to allow the day to own us, so we simply respond to all the competing requests for our time and attention. But doing this usually means we're not consciously focusing on our three lenses of value and what really matters.

There is a simple way to proactively get on top of your daily tasks that contribute toward your bigger goals. It's called the Ivy Lee method.

It started back in 1918 when Charles Schwab was the president of one of the largest companies in the United States at the time, Bethlehem Steel.

Schwab wanted his leaders to be more productive and engaged a consultant by the name of Ivy Lee. During one of their consultations, Lee told Schwab he would need fifteen minutes with each of Bethlehem Steel's senior leaders to talk through his methods. Schwab gave Lee permission and asked how much it would cost. Lee told him, "At the end of the consultation period, in three months, pay me what you think I'm worth." A few months later, Schwab cut Lee a check for US$25,000. That's about US$475,000 in today's money. Not bad for just a short period of work! That's the value of this practical, yet super simple, method.

Like I said, it's really simple to do. But it's also simple to not do. The key is scheduling time into your calendar so you remember to do it each workday.

Here's what Ivy Lee got the leaders to do: At the end of each workday, spend five to ten minutes doing the following things:

1. Write down their six most critical tasks for the next workday. These tasks were the ones that would have the biggest impact or drive the most value.

2. Prioritize them based on which would add the most value. They would place a "1" next to the most important task, a "2" next to the second most important task and so on.

3. The next day, when the leaders started work, start working on task 1 until it was done. Move on to task 2 until done, and then keep going.

4. At the end of the day, the leaders would look at their list and see if there were any tasks still to complete. If so, they would reprioritize these along with any new tasks that came up that day.

5. Repeat.

That's it. So simple, yet so effective.

Of course, there are always things that come up most days. There are urgent meetings, fires to put out, phone calls to answer and much more. How much you can get through your Ivy Lee list depends on your time available throughout each day between meetings, what urgent things pop up, and your ability to focus to accomplish the tasks. It's also not a static list. It's a dynamic list that you work on and can reprioritize throughout your day as needed if more important tasks pop up.

Some clients ask me, "What happens if I can't finish the first item on the list?"

That's entirely possible and that's OK. Maybe you're waiting to hear back from someone about a particular task and they don't respond until the next day. The key is to get as much done as you can before moving on to the next task. Then you can come back to the first task as soon as you can, once you've got what you need back to keep it progressing.

Another question I'm often asked is, "How big should each task be?" The answer is, it's up to you. Consider what you've got going on that day, such as scheduled events already on your calendar, and consider what you can realistically accomplish based on what your day looks like. You can break a big goal into smaller tasks, things you can do in twenty-five minutes or less, and work through them in those bite-sized chunks. As the old saying goes, "How do you eat an elephant? One bite at a time."

As amazing as the Ivy Lee method is, it is over one hundred years old and has room for improvement. Studies now show that people who consistently hit their goals over time are people who set themselves three tasks per day.[28] Achieving your goals reinforces the success mindset because you accomplished everything you wanted to do that day. The more success we experience, the more positive we feel and this in turn leads to more success.

The *Ivy Lee* Method
At the **end** of each day:

✔ Write down your six most critical tasks

✔ Put them in order of priority

✔ When you start work, concentrate on your first task until it's done

✔ Keep going

✔ Move unfinished tasks to the next day's list

✔ Repeat

---

28 - RescueTime, 2018: "Setting Smarter Daily Goals: We Asked Hundreds of RescueTime Users How They Run Their Days," Jory MacKay.

One more question I get asked often is, "Do you use the Ivy Lee method for work or personal tasks?" It can be either.

I personally choose up to three work priorities and up to three personal ones for a twenty-four-hour work period. I blend them throughout the day and evening so that I can accomplish them by the time I go to bed. That works for me. It's about taking the concept and experimenting with what will work best for you.

For example, a personal task might be taking my daughter to the dentist. Or it could be going for a run. In those cases, the dentist gets scheduled into my day just like my work priorities. My run could be before work or during a work break. As mentioned in part 2, a key is "unlearning" that the only viable workweek is nine to five, Monday through Friday. Instead, it's about focusing on work-life integration and working through when it suits for you and your colleagues to get your best work done.

Another thing to think through is how to track your goals in a sustainable way so you can accomplish them consistently over time. I was curious about whether tracking and consistently achieving your goals was more sustainable over time if done with pen and paper, online, or in some other way. It turns out it depends on the individual. In other words, there is no hard-and-fast rule about how you track your goals and your Ivy Lee list. The key is testing and learning which method works best for you, whether it's online, a journal, Post-it Notes, whiteboard, or some other way.

In my case, I have a goals book where I write out my weekly work goals on the left-hand side of the page and my personal goals on the right. At the start of each week, I reflect on my monthly goals, which are written on A3 paper and pinned up on the wall next to my desk, so I can be reminded of them every day.

I call these monthly goals my "big rocks." The original creator of the well-known concept of "big rocks versus pebbles versus sand" is unknown, but is largely attributed to Stephen Covey in his wonderful book *The 7 Habits of Highly Effective People*. My big rocks for each week are my important deliverables (typically aligned with my big rocks for the month) that add the most value for my clients, as well as my nonnegotiables, as outlined in part 1. These are the things I prioritize to do above all else.

At the beginning of each week, I list the most important tasks for that week associated with my big rocks in my weekly goals book. I then look at my online calendar to get clear on when other big deliverables are due. I break them into smaller tasks where needed and schedule them in by day. Next, based on my daily schedule of meetings, coaching and other commitments, I confirm which days I will do my nonnegotiables., I think through when it is realistic for me to go for my runs, when I'll practice yoga, or what I'll do each day to make myself fitter, stronger, and healthier. That gets scheduled in too.

Each day during the week, I then use the Ivy Lee method to review my weekly goals and prioritize my daily tasks, which I refine again at the end of each day for the next workday. This is based on what I've accomplished that day and what new tasks have come in. For my daily Ivy Lee list, I personally use a Post-it Note each day, as I love the feeling of crossing things off my to-do list. It's up to you how you do it—the key is working out what works for you and setting a daily reminder so you don't forget to write out your Ivy Lee list for the next day.

```
MON 19 - SUN 25 JULY

MON : Pip template          5km Run
      TUB Wk 8             →OMLAC Website
      LOLIC H/w              Clean bookcase
      LI Responses          Notebook, pens
                  Slack Email
TUES →Faizan ‹ MS Form      Yoga
      TV
      Prep GE Preso

WED →F/Up OLX              E. PT Interviews
      F/Up Amazon           5km Run
      TV

THURS : Sixteen Thought Piece Post |LI Post w/ CTA
        Clear emails        |Chelle's B'day
      →F/Up ASIC            |Walk
        Boris

FRI : TV                    5km Run
      Send out invoices     A. Dentist
```

My weekly goals book: I keep my top 3 work tasks on the left and personal tasks on the right.

I love crossing items off my to-do lists. I have my annual goals, which are then broken down into a list of smaller goals for the coming quarter, then monthly, weekly and finally, my daily Ivy Lee task list. My monthly goals are on the wall right next to my desk so I can look at them every day. My quarterly goals are in my goals book along with my weekly goals, while my daily goals go on Post-it Notes. This might sound a bit convoluted, but it gives me visibility and clarity at the right level, so I can keep one eye on the long term while dealing with the competing priorities that come in the short to medium term. It's up to you to work out your own style in terms of tracking goals, whether it be online, paper or another method. Whatever works for you to provide clarity and keep you on track of what really matters.

When I have a huge project, I use an online app to manage my tasks or pull out my whiteboard. When a client wants to cocreate a bespoke program with me, I use the whiteboard and employ Agile principles. I write one task each on a Post-it Note and make a column of Post-it Notes listing the tasks in order of priority, similar to the Ivy Lee method. There is a column for the to-do list (the "backlog"), one column for the tasks in progress (the "work in progress" or "WIP"), and one column for tasks that are "done." It's very effective for bigger goals that need to be broken down and delivered with laser-like focus. When working with your remote team, adopting a similar approach online, where you can assign each task by owner, gives you the required clarity, transparency, and accountability.

One of my favorite phrases in business is "fit for purpose." It's about not necessarily working on every goal through a one-size-fits-all lens. Consider which method will help you to deliver the most value in the shortest amount of time? Sometimes it could be using a whiteboard (whether online or physical) and at other times, it might be an app. It could be online or pen and paper. It's all about taking a few moments before starting each goal and thinking through the easiest way to complete it.

What? So what? Now what?

A practical way to bring clarity to your goals is to work through the "What? So what? Now what?" concept, which I learned from one of the biggest organizations in Australia. It works particularly well for large goals that are complex or lack clarity at first. It's not for tasks that are straightforward and you know exactly what to do, like writing an employee's performance appraisal. It's for the big, complex stuff.

The idea is to get clear on the outcomes you and your team are going to deliver (the "What?"), why the outcomes matter (the "So what?"), and the next steps and milestones to be delivered (the "Now what?"). When I ran the projects division at a large, fast-paced organization, one thing I realized was that a lack of clarity would typically lead to annoyed stakeholders. This was because we were not on the same page of exactly what was being delivered. As previously discussed, managing expectations is a core competency of an effective leader—whether remote or not.

The "What?": A lack of clarity of what exactly a project or goal will deliver confuses people. It often involves leaders using jargon, obscure acronyms, and long sentences that seem to go on forever. If you can drill down to what the outcomes will be in one or two sentences using really simple language and terminology that is familiar to anyone in the company, it goes a long way to ensuring everyone can be on the same page. Think about if you showed your goal statement to your local coffee barista in the morning. Would they understand what you're talking about without knowing the ins and outs of the subject matter?

The "So what?": I'm constantly amazed at how often leaders in corporate say what their big work goals are, but when you ask them why they matter, they don't have a strong case supporting the change or articulating the associated benefits. Consider what's going to be better for your team, your customers, or your organization after you spend the resources, time, and money on making the changes. How is fixing that problem or implementing some new technology specifically going to make a difference? Are your employees really wanting the changes you're prioritizing? Your customers? Your organization? Do you have compelling quantitative and qualitative data, feedback, or insights to back this up? It's essential to answer the why question before you assign resources, money, management focus or effort.

The "Now what?": This helps your internal and external stakeholders know what's coming next. What are the high-level tasks to complete to achieve the big audacious goals? When will they be delivered? Who is accountable for making them happen?

This can be a helpful tool, too, when you're establishing your department's annual goals. You might come up with five to ten things that you want your team to accomplish in the next year.

What are they? Remember to use simple language that everyone will understand and keep it concise. So what? Be clear on why those outcomes matter to your people, customers, and organization. Now what? Be clear about what's going to be delivered in the next month or quarter. Share this information widely and readily with your team and relevant stakeholders. Communicate progress with them at regular intervals. This simple exercise goes a long way in rallying your team to focus on what matters most.

What / So What / Now What

WHAT

In 1-2 sentences, using simple language without corporate jargon, what are the big outcomes you will be delivering? Think about if you showed your goal statement to your local coffee barista. Would they understand what you're talking about without knowing the ins and outs of the subject matter?

SO WHAT

How is fixing that specific problem or implementing some new technology specifically going to make a difference? Are your employees really wanting the changes you're prioritizing? Your customers? Your organization? Do you have compelling quantitative and qualitative data or insights to back this up?

NOW WHAT

What are the high-level tasks you need to complete to achieve the big audacious goals? When will they be delivered? Who is accountable for making it happen?

A great tool to get everyone on the same page for big or complex projects and goals.

The "What? So what? Now what?" concept is a way of keeping you and your team accountable while being clear and transparent about what you're doing and bringing everyone on the journey.

Urgent versus important

These days, we throw the word "priority" around like we can have as many of them as we like.

The word priority first came into the English language in England in the 1400s. At that time, the word was singular. Someone might say, "My priority is X." It spoke to the person's prime concern, above all others. The word priority remained singular for about five hundred years. In the 1940s, the word transitioned to being plural and people started saying, "My priorities are ..." I've heard many business leaders say something like, "My top twenty priorities are ..." But to quote Patrick Lencioni, "If everything is important, then nothing is." Many leaders have lost the muscle associated with spending time properly prioritizing before running and jumping into a really long to-do list.

Greg McKeown, in his wonderful book *Essentialism: The Disciplined Pursuit of Less*, writes, "Illogically, we reasoned that by changing the word [priority] we could bend reality."

Leaders often subconsciously reason with themselves that when they change their focus from "priority" to "priorities," they can "bend reality" so that they get more done. Task-switching though makes us less productive. Going from one task to another breaks our concentration and we actually end up taking longer to get things done.[29] Jumping back and forth between competing priorities slows them all down, which also means that value gets into the hands of your people, customers, or organization much later. That's why thinking about your highest *priority* is a good place to start.

This doesn't mean that you only have one goal for the year. In business, that's not realistic. It's about taking the time to think more deeply about the activity that will add the most value and make sense to do right now. If you

---

29 - *Ikagi: The Japanese Secret to a Long and Happy Life* by Hector Garcia and Francesc Miralles.

start with numerous tasks at the same time, and they all move at the same pace, you're going to have fewer high-value tasks completed early.

It's also important to be ruthless about which tasks you start in the first place. And it's OK to put a stop to certain tasks or projects that are not as high a priority, particularly if the context or external environment changes.

Day to day, many new tasks come on our radar demanding our time. Constantly reprioritizing is an essential skill as a leader. The Eisenhower matrix is an effective tool to help with this. Chances are, the former United States president Dwight Eisenhower had a lot more tasks come across his desk each day than you or I do. To deal with so many competing requests for his time and focus, he created a simple yet effective system to decide which tasks he should prioritize each day.

In Eisenhower's first quadrant are the tasks considered important and urgent. These are given the highest priority and should be completed first. I've found that business leaders are pretty good at prioritizing and completing these tasks. We're skilled at dropping everything when something critical pops up that really matters and we put out the fire. Most of my clients agree. These are not the tasks that challenge them to focus on or get done. They're challenged much more by tasks that fall in the other three quadrants.

The most challenging tasks to complete for most of my clients are those considered important but not urgent. However, Eisenhower categorizes these as the second most important tasks to complete. These are things like taking time as a team to create a compelling vision, prioritizing your own personal development, coaching team members, reflecting on how your team is progressing toward meeting their goals, and looking after yourself. Leaders often think these tasks don't really matter whether they happen today, next week, or next month. They're easy to push out when someone is demanding your time right now. But focusing on tasks in this quadrant can produce positive micro-habits and make an incredible difference. The solution is to schedule these tasks into your calendar, so you can put aside time to work on and complete them effectively.

The third most important category is tasks that are urgent, but not necessarily important and worthy of your time. These are tasks to either delegate to someone else or push back on having them on your to-do list in the first place.

The final category consists of the tasks that are not important and not urgent. These tasks are the ones to avoid at all costs. I'm a huge fan of "to-do" lists, but I'm also a big fan of "to-don't" lists. Items that fall into this final quadrant are ones to commit to NOT doing, so you can declutter your mind—and not feel guilty about it.

To-don't lists, that is, considering what is out of your scope, are just as important as to-do lists. When I was the director of projects for a large organization, we'd often put together a scoping document to spell out the parameters of a project. As much as I loved this process of making it super clear what we were working on, my team and stakeholders got nearly as much value out of the section of the document that spelled out the out-of-scope deliverables. Our most robust conversations often came from that section of the file, because someone would invariably say, "I thought we were going to do A, B, and C, but I see them listed in the out-of-scope section. Are we really not doing them?" That was the perfect opportunity to have the difficult conversation up front about why those deliverables were not deemed as important. To make the implicit explicit.

This tool helps you understand which tasks are urgent versus important.

We often avoid a tough five-minute conversation up front when asked to complete a task. Informing the people relying on us that we won't get to a certain task because other things are deemed to drive more value for our team, customers, or organization might feel awkward at first, but managing expectations well will always win out in the long run.

I learned this powerful lesson on managing expectations many years ago through reviewing the insights from one company's net promoter score (NPS) data. The general NPS question is *"On a scale from one to ten, where ten is the highest, how likely are you to recommend [company's] products and services to others?"* The data is then used to assess how likely an organization's customers are to recommend the company's products and services to others as well as why.

A customer who ranks your company a nine or ten out of ten is considered a "promoter," which means they are more likely to rave to their friends and family about your company. They love your products and services and will become your best evangelists. Customers who give scores of seven or eight are called "passives." These people like your company, but they won't drive the growth of your brand through word of mouth.

Customers who score your company one to six are called "detractors." They've had a poor experience and are likely to tell others about it, which inhibits your company's growth.

Many years ago, I worked with a large organization that was researching its detractors. They wanted to understand why certain customers didn't like their products and services. A core service provided by the company was to provide payouts to customers who made insurance claims, knowing that their customers wanted their refunds in their bank account as soon as possible.

Two distinct groups of customers emerged, based on their NPS scores. One group of customers were told their refunds would take twenty-one days to land in their accounts, but on average, only took fourteen. However, a second group of customers was told their refunds would only take two days, but on average, took five. Interestingly, the first group of customers gave a much higher NPS score on average, despite getting their refunds in their accounts on average nine days later than the second group. Despite their comparatively faster turnaround times, which most customers cared about, this second group was much more likely to be made up of detractors. Put simply, they felt let down because their expectations hadn't been appropriately managed.

As I would often say to my teams, "No surprises." It relates back to Brené Brown's quote, too, "Clarity is kind." Having up-front conversations about priorities and managing expectations. That's how you build credibility and great relationships in business. Getting crystal clear first about your big vision and then what it is you want to accomplish annually, quarterly, monthly, weekly, and daily will help you to optimize the impact of the Eisenhower matrix. An hour here and there focused on strategic planning usually saves hours down the track, whether that be from rework, focusing on tasks that aren't aligned with your vision, or on things that just aren't that important.

Leveraging the Eisenhower matrix, all the known, important tasks and meetings are scheduled into your diary. These typically are a mix of urgent and nonurgent tasks. Urgent ones, such as meeting a deadline for submitting the company's annual report, need to be given the highest level of importance. These are followed by the important yet nonurgent tasks, such as strategic thinking time, coaching team members, or self-development.

Once you have all your important items in your diary, you can assess your daily schedule. Chances are, you're going to get things thrown at you from left field, issues you weren't expecting. In real time, you must analyze the requests to see if they're important or urgent. But start with the basic building block of scheduling in your important tasks first.

As things come your way throughout the day, filter them through your lens of importance—the Eisenhower matrix. Triage them and only schedule them in if they fall in an important quadrant. If important, do it right away or schedule it in. If it's not, either delegate to a team member or have the up-front conversation to manage expectations.

Keep asking yourself, "What is my first, my primary, concern?" There are times when urgent issues pop up and push everything else to the side. That's OK. But think it through consciously and ask yourself each time, "Is this really more important than that?" If you've already got important tasks baked into your diary, when something important and urgent comes up, where do you push those other important tasks so you can focus on the new priority?

This happens all the time when you lead a team, whether remote or not. I learned a simple solution to address this from a chief risk officer (CRO) I worked closely with. Make room in your calendar every day for urgent items to pop up. Chances are you know they're going to come up, even if you don't know exactly what or when. It's not a surprise that urgent issues bounce in most days, or that important matters pop up. For most leaders, it happens weekly, if not daily. The CRO's practical solution is to schedule in your calendar most days a couple of floating hours during the day where urgent matters can be dealt with. You won't know what those are at the start of the day, but expect them to come up and when they do, you've already got time on your schedule to be able to deal with them.

I've found that having two hours of free time daily in my diary is optimal, even if not realistic every single day. If something urgent comes up, I've got it covered. If nothing urgent comes up, terrific! I've got that time for thinking, dreaming, creating, or other important tasks.

Building empty time into your calendar so you can deal with the unforeseen fires that need to be put out or focus on unexpected but important work can free you up in several ways. Bill Gates and Warren Buffett are considered two of the most successful business leaders of all time. Interestingly, Gates is known for not having back-to-back meetings every day on his calendar. Buffett is famously known for only having a few meetings scheduled in his calendar each week. They both ensure they have lots of time to think, reflect, and do their best work. Having a jam-packed diary does not set you up for success, because you know there are going to be things that will be thrown at you each day. It's important to have buffers to give yourself room to breathe.

So, start with the important tasks scheduled in and build into your diary some buffer time. Next, all the other work that comes across your desk. This is the unimportant stuff, or what I call noise. These are the things that are easy to attract your time and energy even though they're probably not going to drive the best value for your people, customers, or organization. This is when you really need to triage. To think through and recognize what is important and what is not important. Some things just aren't a great use of your time.

If you come across a task or request that isn't a good use of your time, work through how to quickly get it out of your head and off your plate. Does it make sense to delegate it to someone on your team? Or is it something that just isn't that critical to be done at all? In these instances, you may need to have a conversation where you say, "Sorry, this just isn't a priority right now."

I contacted many executives to invite them to be interviewed for this book. Luckily, many saw sharing their insights with you as important and so made the time for me to interview them. However, as expected, three of them said no. Here are their rejection emails:

Rejection Email 1:

Hi Tina,

Thanks for your note and for thinking of me, but I will pass on this occasion.

Regards,

[Name]

Rejection Email 2:

Hi Tina,

Thanks for your email; however, this is not an opportunity that I would like to pursue.

All the best,

[Name]

Rejection Email 3:

Hi Tina,

Thanks for reaching out! The topic you are addressing is super relevant and hits home in this current climate we are in. I'm currently caught up with a number of commitments at work and will not be able to commit to this. All the best with your book and success with this!

Regards,

[Name]

Simple, kind and straight to the point.

Back to Brené Brown: "Clarity is kind."

Having a quick conversation or sending a polite response like the ones above and managing expectations is one of the most useful skills for effective leaders. Ensure there are no surprises. Be sure no one else is counting on you or your team for something that you don't intend to deliver. When you have this conversation up front, it means you're not letting someone down. It builds trust. You're also super clear about your priorities. Either delegate or have that up-front conversation.

As items come in throughout the day, go through the triage process and in your mind, quickly assign a level of importance to each task or activity. If it's important, schedule or do it right away based on its level of urgency. If it's urgent, you've got buffer time built into your daily calendar to deal with it. If it's not urgent, find a place for it over the coming weeks or months. If it's not important and you need it off your plate, delegate it or say no. If it doesn't warrant the attention of someone on your team, then have the up-front conversation.

Many of my clients ask how to best handle when the requests come from your boss or another senior leader. The best solution I've found is to be transparent about what I've prioritized above the task I'm saying no to or not now. I'll generally say something like, "Here are my five most important things I'm focused on completing this week. I don't think this new request you've asked me to do is more important than any of these—do you agree?" This gives them the opportunity to understand all the important work that has been prioritized and have a say. There are times when it will need to be added to your to-do list (remember the "peaks and troughs" concept!) but often can lead to your boss understanding why it won't get done right now.

Adaptive leadership

If employees do their best work when they have control over where and when they do it, you're going to fall behind by not getting in step with the trend. For many leaders, this means unlearning some of the things that have made them successful up until now. What got most of them to senior positions within their company? It was usually hard work, long hours, and being seen in the office. It was sitting down with the boss at 7 p.m. and saying, "I'm still working on that report. I'll leave when it's done." If they needed to leave the office at 5 p.m., they would leave their jacket hung over the back of their chair so it looked like they were still there.

Being the office hero and working those long hours was a badge of honor for many leaders and ambitious upcomers. Their attitude was similar to Gordon Gekko's, the character in the movie *Wall Street*, who said, "Lunch is for wimps." That mentality was rewarded and people got promotions based on it.

When you think about that, it's understandable why certain leaders might say, "Hang on! I went through that. That's what made me successful. And that's also how I'll continue to lead." However, times change. And when the winds change direction, it's wise to take note and readjust your sails appropriately. To succeed in this new-normal corporate world, leaders must "unlearn" some of the concepts that have made them successful to date. As Charles Darwin famously said, "*It is not the strongest of the species that survives, nor the most intelligent that survives. It is the one that is most adaptable to change.*" Adapt or say goodbye to career progression.

There's a wonderful book by Greg McKeown titled *Effortless: Make It Easier to Do What Matters Most.* He writes that a task being labeled as easy is often associated with the person performing it being lazy. We have this notion that great work must be hard work. Think of the sayings "I gave it my blood, sweat, and tears" and "no pain, no gain." But great work doesn't always have to require a lot of effort. If we can work out a way so that the same task is made easier but produces the same outcome, then we should celebrate that.

If we look at a task that might take thirty hours to complete, we can ask ourselves, "What would this look like if it were effortless? How would we tackle this task if it were *easy*?"

This requires a mindset shift and unlearning that great outcomes must require long hours. Or as one executive at Microsoft told me, "*Great leaders role model to their teams to focus on impact over activity.*" Instead of constantly focusing on the effort, we focus more on the outcomes. I'm not saying that effort isn't important—hard work is still a critical part of the success equation, particularly when obstacles come up that make the work harder to get done—it's just not the only thing. Giving your team the freedom to choose how, when, and where they approach their hard work will lead to better employee engagement and outcomes. If you can do the work effectively and efficiently and get better results, that's great.

This thinking leaves behind the command-and-control approach and makes room for the trust-your-team approach. But you have to make sure that you have set a clear vision and the outcomes you want delivered, particularly as you aren't discussing them face-to-face with your team in the office every day. What are the metrics? What does "done" look like for key deliverables? What are the nonnegotiable company values employees need to demonstrate in reaching the outcomes? What are the team rules around how to collaborate when working remotely together? Being clear on the answers to these questions gives your team the guardrails to work within as you give them more freedom, knowing they will not always be in your sight.

Effective leaders understand that success is a result of inspiring a team of people to do meaningful work together, aligned with a clear vision. That work reflects directly on you. Therefore, if you can free your team up to do their best work in the most effective and efficient way, the way they want to do it, that is better for your success and career as well as theirs.

To quote the old sport's adage, "A champion team will always beat a team of champions."

Remember, they're grown-ups! Let them work out how they work best, including how they work best together as a remote team. Creating the time and space for these conversations is not only important, but it's often urgent too.

My burnout was the catalyst for these conversations with my team. Working on that special project with my company's CEO and burning out made me realize that I had the seeds of a new way to work inside me but they needed to come to the surface. It changed the way I worked. Even though I had been focused on outcomes, there were constantly many more outcomes I felt I needed to deliver. I had my day job and a special project to do. That meant the number of outcomes and the magnitude of the outcomes increased significantly, without consciously reassessing what was now most urgent and important based on my workload doubling. I literally just put my head down to try to deliver it all. Hello, pneumonia. Going through that time flipped a switch inside me. I changed my thinking to relentlessly focus on achieving the most valuable outcomes and not necessarily focusing on everything that came across my desk. Easy doesn't necessarily mean lazy.

In my twenties, I'd worked one-hundred-hour weeks. Literally.

I was groomed in the school of hard work. People would say to me, "You've sold your soul to the devil."

Working one-hundred-hour weeks meant I got to travel the world on the company's dime. But I didn't have a life. I didn't have time to look after myself.

I wouldn't trade that time in my life though for anything. I made some amazing friends who are now scattered all around the world. I learned a lot, but I was always sprinting. Keeping that sort of pace up for decades isn't realistic. To expect that others do that the same for me when I became a leader just because I had done it just didn't make sense to me.

For one thing, anyone who continues to work at that pace will miss out on whole areas of their life that could be amazing. For some, this could mean missing out on having dinner at home with their family most nights. For others, it might mean they'd miss out on being able to go for a run at 4 p.m. or surf at the beach when the waves were up. They could miss out on the opportunity to explore new restaurants with friends or see a new play opening in town.

Work can be a huge source of fulfillment. However, having a successful career isn't mutually exclusive to having a great life outside of work.

Another reason I'm sold on giving employees the freedom to work remotely is that I'm a huge fan of the saying, "Pay it forward."

If your corporate life has been a hard slog for you, do you really want that for other people? Deep down, is that really what you want others to go through just because you did? If you could create a legacy for the next generation of leaders, would you inspire them to lead in a different way so that they don't have to go through what you went through? It could be an amazing legacy to leave, showing emerging talent how to have similar work success to what you have had by traveling a different path. Why cut off your nose to spite your face when you can teach the next generation to achieve far more with less effort? Imagine the impact you could leave, not only on those leaders, but on their loved ones and the next generation of employees, as well.

When you hire the right people, you trust that they're going to do a great job. They, in turn, don't feel like they must show you everything they're doing. They can focus on their most valuable work. There's something to be said for leaders who understand that if your team is showing you everything they're doing, then they don't feel empowered. They're wasting their time and yours.

I've seen senior leaders in many organizations "do business with themselves." Numerous internal approvals. Having a "meeting before the meeting" to make sure people's real concerns are understood in a one-on-one setting before having the big group meeting. Making beautiful eighty-page Power-Point presentations that will never be seen by anyone outside the company. If you and your colleagues are spending the majority of your time doing business with yourselves, it's your customers who miss out.

We live in a time where information is accessible everywhere. It's right at our fingertips. We have our smartphones in our hands most of the time. We don't need more information. We need it filtered and distilled into the most important pieces.

Working with several chief information officers, chief operating officers, and chief technology officers has taught me that data is something many companies can point to as a competitive advantage, but only if it is used intelligently. Having more information is just quantity. It clutters up people's minds. What's important is the insights you gain from the information. One powerful insight from data is worth so much more than ten graphs of data that you don't do anything with. It's about being very deliberate about what you and your team look at, the questions you ask, and the insights you gain rather than simply consuming information.

The Pareto principle

Some people are proud of the number of hours they work. They wear the word "busy" like a badge of honor. They may work one hundred hours every week because they're really committed to their job. To them, all hours appear equal. But they're not. Working smarter is about quality over quantity. And as Debbie Millman says, "*Busy is a decision.*"

I'm a big fan of the Pareto principle as a foundation of working smarter. It's also known as the 80/20 rule.

Vilfredo Pareto was an Italian economist at the turn of the twentieth century. He realized that 20 percent of his peas produced 80 percent of his total crop. This concept has been adopted and adapted in many ways in the business world. Leaders leverage Pareto's insights to find out which processes in their companies drive the most value. They'll likely find that a small percent of the processes drive the biggest proportion of value.

I used the 80/20 principle a lot in my Lean Six Sigma roles at work. When I analyzed core business processes, I'd look at the data and ask, "Where are the biggest benefits? What are our processes, customer segments, contact channels, and costs that have the biggest impact on our overall business metrics?" Using statistical analysis, we discovered that not every task we did had equal value. For me, working smarter means finding that 20 percent. Finding those activities where, if you focus your time on them, you'll have an unfair advantage in achieving the biggest results. Then, the focus is to strip away as much of the other 80 percent of activity that might make you feel good, make you feel busy and important, but it doesn't really make that much of a difference.

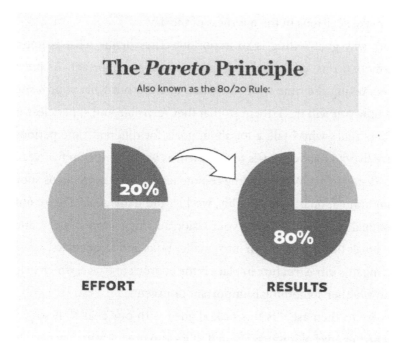

Working harder often seems to hinge on focusing on trying to get more done, but that doesn't always equate with adding more value. Answering more emails. Attending more meetings. Starting work earlier and finishing later. Pushing harder. Instead of focusing on the inputs—how many hours you work, how many emails you respond to, how many meetings you attend, how quickly you respond to messages—focus on the outputs. In other words, ask the question, "What are the outcomes in my role that will make the biggest impact?" Not all tasks deliver the same amount of value.

This exercise trains your mind to not be reactive. Just because someone else thinks a task demands your attention or considers it a priority doesn't mean that you must see it that way. Remember your role and the value you bring to your team, your customers, and your organization.

The only way triage works is if you're clear on what matters in the first place. If you're clear on your vision, overall goals, and KPIs, then triage works.

If you're not clear on your "North Star" and where your team's value is, it's very hard to make decisions in the busyness of the day.

That's why goal setting is so important. They define what is important. With remote teams, clear goals become even more important. As previously discussed, taking the time with your team to work out what your team goals are and how you will track them so that they're visible and super clear is time well spent. That's why I talk a lot about goals for different time periods. You may have five- to ten-year goals for yourself, as well as three- to five-year goals for your department. When leading remote teams, even more focus should go into your annual, quarterly, monthly, weekly, and daily goals. Figure out your team's annual goals, aligned with your vision and long-term strategy, and then you can break those goals down into smaller tasks and frequencies.

Having this infrastructure in place is the bedrock of triage, which helps you work out whether something is important or urgent.

It's easy to then ask, "Is this task aligned with our goals?" If so, you can assign a higher level of importance to it. If it's also urgent, you may need to rally your team and delegate some other tasks to get it done.

Retrospectives

An extra step I encourage people to work through is completing a "retrospective," which you'll often hear referred to as a "retro." The term comes from Agile ways of working. It's about reflecting on the past and learning from it so you can improve for the future. The three key questions to ask as a team are:

1. "What went well?"
2. "How can we improve?"
3. "What did we learn?"

Several companies schedule regular retros for their Agile teams or specific project teams. I encourage you to also build retros into all teams' regular operating rhythms.

I personally go through the retro exercise every month. I reflect on how I am going as a leader and where I can improve. I also encourage my clients to do this simple exercise, to reflect on the past month and ask themselves, "Did I achieve my goals?" "What went well and what didn't?" and "What have I learned, so that I can improve for next month?" The more we understand what goes well at work and why, the more we can learn so we can replicate the wins and deliver similar outcomes. Chip and Dan Heath, in their book *Switch: How to Change Things When Change Is Hard*, refer to looking for the "bright spots" in your organization. That is, understanding what's working well so you can model it. Often leaders focus on what's not working. However, it's just as relevant to reflect on what you want to keep doing more of as a leader and team.

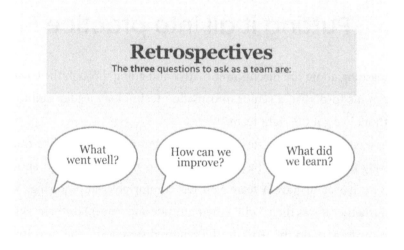

Retrospectives: a simple tool to use with your team so you can continuously improve your ways of working and outcomes together.

If you want more success, look for the things that made you successful in the past. Take these learnings into the next month and at the end of that month, go through the retro exercise again to see what you have since learned. Each month, reflect on what you have learned in working toward your goals and ask yourself, "How can I keep getting better at hitting my goals each month?"

This also helps you improve your goal setting and estimating so they are more realistic for future months. This time for reflection creates the space for you to work through how to best "chunk" your goals down into smaller tasks that can easily be scheduled into your calendar.

When you set your goals, it's important that they're not set and forgotten. I've seen many people write their goals and KPIs for the year, then when it's time for their performance appraisal, they pull them out to remember what they'd written all those months ago. Breaking down goals and KPIs into smaller time frames and tasks, with ongoing visibility and tracking, creates transparency, clarity, and accountability. These are critical elements for leading an effective remote team.

Putting it all into practice

After learning about the Eisenhower matrix and going through the triage exercise with his to-do list, a senior information technology leader said to me, "I don't think I've got the right team."

He was trying to delegate a lot to them, but he didn't feel like they were effectively delivering what he was assigning to them. We talked about how important it was to have a team you felt comfortable empowering. We discussed whether it was their "will" (their attitude and values) or their "skill" (did they know how to do the work to the required standard?) that was impeding them. The leader's shoulders dropped when he replied, "It's their skill. They're a great bunch; I just haven't taught them how to do higher-order work." On the surface, it didn't seem urgent to do anything differently. The leader could get through the day to day doing most tasks himself. But, if he did nothing to address these issues, in twelve months, he would still be at the same place he was now. He wouldn't be making meaningful progress to effectively deliver on his department's ambitions. He realized that if he didn't spend time coaching his team and dealing with the lower performers, then nothing was going to change.

That realization was the starting point for him in understanding the importance of increasing the "C" ("coaching") in his SCD (strategy, coaching & leadership, doing) ratio. He told me, "I need to build the capabilities in my team so that I can delegate more to them. Then I can focus on the more strategic work and things only I can do."

The light bulb came on!

By building up his team, everyone would win. This concept of focusing on what the team needed from him so that they could collaborate effectively and deliver their most valuable work, the concept of servant leadership, is not new. However, it's even more critical for remote teams who rely on the micro-moments of interacting with their boss and colleagues to determine whether trust and connection are preserved.

This IT leader was able to triage his tasks into the correct quadrant and manage them based on their importance and urgency. There were some tasks that he realized that needed to be taken care of before they reached the urgent level. They were currently important, but not urgent. He realized he didn't want them to become urgent, knowing that if the tasks got to that stage, they would usually take a lot more hours to complete. We talked a lot about building in time for strategic reviews of his team's capabilities. We looked at his team, what they were capable of today, where they needed to grow, and assessed how much time he would free up in the future by focusing on coaching his team today.

This exercise helped that leader realize that his leadership team was, in fact, the right one and had helped him be successful up to that point in time. But to get to the next level, he was going to have to do some more intensive coaching. Their current skills wouldn't get the team where they wanted to go in the future and deliver on their vision.

It starts with evaluating your team's capabilities. What roles do they play? What are they great at? What can you always rely on them for? Where do you feel you might be micromanaging them and why? Particularly when you aren't face-to-face with your team every day, understanding what will give you the comfort level to trust and empower your team is time well spent. Identify those areas and then set a plan for coaching your team members to develop the skills necessary to help your team reach their goals. That might require you personally coaching them, assigning them a business coach or putting them through development courses that will give them the skills they need.

Financial literacy was one skill that came up for this leader's team. He needed them to be able to understand how finance works: to understand the company's profit and loss (P&L) statement and balance sheet, as well as to understand what their profitability drivers were, so that they could make better decisions on behalf of the company. He needed them to build their commercial acumen. He reflected on what each team member needed in order to build this capability. Who just needed a bit of help here and there? Who needed more dedicated coaching and did it make sense for that coaching to come from someone other than him? Who, upon serious reflection, did he feel would never get there?

This exercise led to some tough conversations. Most team members rose to the occasion relatively quickly. Others needed dedicated coaching on a regular basis as well as external training to get there.

This leader also leveraged the power of the Pareto principle in hiring new team members. Hire a committed, loyal, and talented team member once and you reap the rewards thousands of times over. Previously, recruiting was a painstaking process for him. But the Pareto principle helped him see this as a vitally important task that delivered significant benefits. Getting the right people into the right roles might be time-consuming up front, but it pays back in spades over time. Once new team members have settled in, they require much less of your time to coach, while the high levels of trust help cut through time following up or second-guessing what they are working on.

He could have filled his roles quickly, but he realized that if he did, it would come back to haunt him. This would have done more damage over time when he needed to delegate to the new team members. Any short-term gain would be more damaging due to the longer-term consequences.

In the end, he was pleased that he invested his time in hiring the right people. As he put it, "I focused on getting the right people, realizing how important it was, versus making quick, tactical decisions and having the wrong people in my team. This has freed me up tremendously to focus on the things that only I can do."

CHAPTER 9

Free Up Time to Reinvest

"I'm in back-to-back meetings from eight to five most days. Then my real work can start."

—Senior leader and client

The more we accomplish, the better we usually feel about what we're doing. The better we feel, the more productive we become. This, in turn, leads to more success. As the soccer great Mia Hamm says, *"Success breeds success."* So, the more efficiently we can get through things that matter, the more we can accomplish and move on to driving even more value for our teams, our customers, and our organizations.

It's a simple formula: once you're super clear on what needs to be done, if you can get through it faster, it frees up your time to focus on the next most important thing.

A real sense of accomplishment comes from getting things done and getting them done faster. This only matters, though, if you've gone through the steps to make sure you are working on the right things in the first place. There's no point being super efficient and getting through things quickly if they're the wrong things to focus on in the first place. Therefore, it's important to first go through the step of focusing on the "what." What you are going to deliver needs to be thought through appropriately before you focus on the "how."

Your 168 hours

Freeing up time to reinvest is one of my favorite concepts because clients usually come to me when they're overwhelmed. Often they feel so busy that they struggle to prioritize the time to schedule an initial call with me, even though they know it's their ticket to freeing up time for themselves and their team to get back in control.

Many business leaders think there's no good way to free up time, but I love this subject because when they discover my strategies and that they can do it, it's usually life-changing for them. The reason freeing up time is important is that leaders know they typically work a lot of hours in a week. It's not like corporate leaders sit on the beach, working just two hours a day. But in the hours that you do work, there's an opportunity to look at your time differently, so you can free up time to reinvest your hours in the activities that matter most to you. This may include focusing on tasks that will add significant value to your people, customers, or organization. It may involve spending time with your family or doing something that inspires you. The idea is to free yourself of feeling like a hamster chasing itself on the wheel of corporate work.

After my own burnout, I spent a great deal of time reflecting on how I let myself get to that stage. I analyzed how I spent my time in the lead-up to my burnout. It was an impactful exercise, and it's been impactful for thousands of my clients around the world ever since. It's all about being conscious about where you choose to spend your time.

We all have twenty-four hours in a day and seven days a week. If you do the math, that gives us all 168 hours every week. To keep the math simple, let's say you work fifty hours a week and sleep a bit more than seven hours a night, which equates to another fifty hours in your week. Work and sleep then total about one hundred hours a week. That leaves you with another sixty-eight hours for all of your other things each week.

When I share this concept with my clients, the first thing they typically say to me is, "I can probably account for about thirty of those sixty-eight other hours. But I have no idea where those other thirty-eight hours go!"

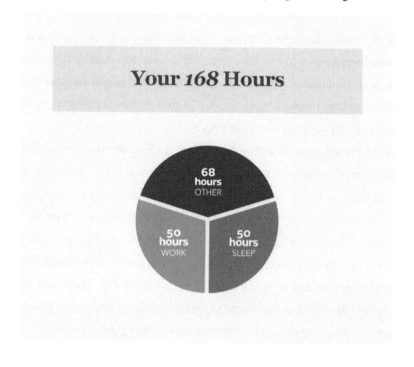

Your 168 hours: a practical concept to analyze where you spend your time and find opportunities to free up time to reinvest.

As a certified Master Black Belt in Lean Six Sigma, I've been trained to analyze the current state of key business processes in order to understand their strengths and weaknesses, evaluate the relevant data, and discover where the most impactful opportunities are to transform the business. Translating a similar approach to people, I encourage my clients to reflect on their own 168 hours in a typical week. I get them to analyze where they spend their time and think through where they have "wasted hours," based on their own definition, that they might want to reinvest.

A really important point here is how you define "wasted hours." Your definition is completely up to you, based on what you consider to be wasted time.

Some people enjoy coming home from work, sitting on the couch, and watching TV for a few hours. If that helps you unwind and you feel great about it, go for it. However, if you spend all night watching movies and find yourself feeling like there's more to life, then you might want to consider if some of that time could be considered in your "wasted hours." You might want to do something else with that time going forward. The first step in the process is to audit your 168 hours in a typical week for you.

When I played around with this concept for the first time about a decade ago, I was experimenting. I was trying to understand how I spent my time. I found that there were two areas in my life in particular where I was wasting lots of time in a way that didn't serve me or my family well. When I share these two areas with my clients, they often tell me they struggle in the same areas. Working with my clients over time, it's typical that they free up the equivalent of half to one whole day a week in those two areas, just like I did. They then reinvest their time in ways that make them happier, healthier, and more productive. That's a pretty amazing return on investment for doing this exercise!

One of my clients, a chief technology officer (CTO), found about nine hours a week when he first went through this exercise. He was gobsmacked. Then he began to consider what he could do with those nine hours. Fast forward a few months and he had revamped his CTO strategy with his team, invested heavily in coaching his leadership team, and consistently found time to look after himself.

So what are the two areas that seem to be the "Bermuda Triangle of time" for many corporate leaders?

Meeting madness

The first category that is a common problem for my clients around the world, irrespective of the company they work for or the country they live in, is what I call "meeting madness." It's the percent of our workweek that we spend in meetings. And those meetings are usually back-to-back with no breaks in between. We press "leave" on one online meeting and within thirty seconds have clicked "join" on the next. In the office, team members drop by your desk to say hi for five minutes. But with the shift to remote teams, that's been replaced by constant thirty- and sixty-minute meetings throughout the work-day. In fact, back-to-back meetings are the norm. A lot of people have accepted it as normal that they'll be in meetings from eight to five and then their "real work" can begin.

That's a lot of time to spend in meetings. It's worth considering whether they are all meetings that you really need to attend. Leaders have reported that 83 percent of the meetings in their calendar were unproductive and US-based professionals have rated meetings as the "number one office productiv-ity killer."[30]

When I first analyzed my 168 hours, I realized that I wasted two to four hours most days in meetings that I really didn't need to be in, for a whole host of reasons.

It started with a mindset shift. Before, when meeting invites landed in my inbox, I'd accept all of them straight away. Sometimes, this meant that my calendar was double- or triple-booked. Then I would have to decide which meeting I would attend and decline the others at the last minute. So much for my philosophy of "no surprises!" It had never occurred to me that perhaps I shouldn't even attend any of them. Now, I think about meeting invites in the same way I think about party invites.

---

30 - "The Psychology Behind Meeting Overload," Ashley Whillans, Dave Feldman, and Damian Wisniewski, *Harvard Business Review*, 2021.

When you get an invitation to a party, you know that you've got a choice about attending. You think it through consciously and ask yourself, "Do I want to accept this invitation?" Maybe you don't really want to go and you politely decline. I took that mindset into my work meetings. Now, when I get a meeting invite, I go through the same mental exercise. I ask myself if I really need to be at the meeting and, if not, whether I will accept or decline the invite.

I established some parameters to help me decide which meetings I would go to and which invites I would decline. I reviewed my diary and saw how many meetings I had scheduled in my diary that were recurring meetings. Many of them had generic meeting titles, something like "Weekly catch-up with Tina." Some were weekly and some were biweekly, but they didn't have a reason for "catching up" other than the meeting invites came from important stakeholders, team members, or other executives. "Catching up" on a regular basis made sense though in the context of building or maintaining a good working relationship. However, I realized that these thirty- or sixty-minute meetings might not be the best use of their time or mine. So I examined the frequency of the meetings and asked myself if the weekly catch-up meetings could be biweekly and if the biweekly ones could be pushed out to monthly.

Secondly, I considered the duration of the recurring meetings. Did I really need to meet for an hour every time for a "catch up" meeting? Where practical, I shortened them to twenty-five minutes so that we could have a five-minute break before inevitably the next meeting was scheduled. If they were thirty minutes, I'd look to shorten them where I could to fifteen minutes.

While working through this process, I wanted to make sure the person I wanted to have a strong connection with didn't feel that they were no longer important to me or the work we were doing together. Before making the changes, I sent them each an email saying something like:

"Hi _____, I know your time is precious and you're probably booked in back-to-back meetings, as am I. I want to free up time for both of us, so I'm pushing out our regular catch-ups from weekly to biweekly and changing them from one hour to twenty-five minutes."

The next sentence I wrote in the message, though, was the most important one:

"If something important comes up though in between our regular catch-ups, please just drop me a note or book in an extra meeting so that we can keep things moving. Thanks, Tina."

That way, they knew they could always catch up with me on critical issues in a timely manner.

There's a wonderful rule called Parkinson's law. Cyril Parkinson was a British historian who wrote that *"work expands to fill the time allotted for its completion."*

I got to put Parkinson's law into practice a few years ago while working for a large multinational organization. Every month, the CEO, the executive, and I would discuss all the big projects being worked on across the company. These meetings would last for four hours every month until one month the CEO said to me, "Tina, I want to limit these meetings to two hours each month."

We had a lot of important projects to talk about, so I wasn't convinced it was possible. However, when I started planning the agenda for the meeting each month, the most important work bubbled to the surface and everything else fell away. We got better at discussing the strategic priorities and delegating the rest.

Since then, I've carried this philosophy into every work project and task. For meetings, I look at the frequency, duration, and necessity. If it doesn't meet my criteria, it doesn't get my attention. If it gets my attention, it gets only the amount of attention necessary to get the job done. If it doesn't require my attention but is necessary for my team to do a good job, then it gets delegated.

Building on this concept, my team and I implemented another general rule for meetings. If one person from our team was also invited to the same meeting, then only one of us went. We would represent each other and our team.

This often led to a quick five-minute conversation. One of us would ask, "Does it make more sense for you or for me to attend that workshop?" We'd decide which one of us would represent our team. If there were important points we wanted to be made, we'd share them with the person attending the meeting and they'd convey the other person's opinions. If I attended, I'd collect the inputs from my colleagues and share them in the meeting. After the meeting, whoever attended would brief the relevant team members by email or at our next team meeting.

This framework we developed as a team for meetings freed up a lot of time because we realized how often we were doing business with ourselves.

We focused on being clear on the objectives for our meetings. There are too many meetings in corporate where people show up only to ask, "What's this meeting about?" No one is clear. When a meeting invite hit my inbox and it wasn't crystal clear what the meeting was about, I'd tentatively accept and ask, "Can you please let me know what this meeting is about?" If it still wasn't clear after getting a response, I'd follow up with "Can you please let me know what specifically you need from me for this meeting, or if it's something we can quickly cover off via email?"

Meeting *Madness*

5 questions to ask yourself before accepting a meeting invite:

1. Recurring meetings: Can I change the *duration/frequency?*

2. Is there a *clear objective* for this meeting?

3. Do they really need *me?*

4. Is someone else from *my team* also invited?

5. Could we reach the same objective in *less* time?

Use these simple questions to help you determine which meetings make sense for you to accept and which to decline.

Spending five to ten minutes thinking through this process can save fifty minutes sitting in an hour-long meeting that might not actually be the best use of your time.

Social media

The second area where my clients and I found we could free up a lot of time was social media.

Before my burnout, at night, I'd sit down to scroll through social media on my phone for five minutes, but five minutes would quickly turn into an hour. Then, two hours later, I'd still be there scrolling.

Between meetings, I'd quickly check my social media to fill the void of those two minutes. I didn't have any downtime. The number of times I'd check on social media throughout the day was staggering. The amount of time I spent on social media was bad enough, but the frequency that I checked on it was also significant. With our smartphones with us for most of our waking hours, it's too easy to check our phones at the first moment of peace and quiet.

Most phones have a screen time app that allows you to see how long you've been on each of the apps that you use. You can also see how frequently you engage with them. When I analyzed my 168 hours, I discovered just how much time I spent on social media. I saw loads of "wasted hours," based on my definition, per week. I decided to make a change.

I realized I didn't want to engage with social media for hours at a time. I wanted to be able to quickly check it a few times a week, but I found it hard to stop scrolling once I started. And it was too easy to simply pick up my phone and check it at my first moment of downtime. The amount of time and how often I checked my accounts made me annoyed with myself, particularly when I knew it was often at the expense of getting enough sleep or prioritizing going for a run.

When I saw how much time I was wasting on social media, I knew there were solutions I could find to reduce my usage. The overarching question I now ask myself when I pick up my phone is, "Why am I picking up my phone right now?" Is it for a deliberate reason, such as to check my work emails, call someone, or send a message? Is it simply because I'm bored? Is it because I have a few minutes in between meetings and I'm just filling in time, when I could instead take this moment to stretch my legs or take some deep breaths? Asking myself this simple question has stopped me numerous times from checking my phone "just because."

The most effective way to reduce your social media time, albeit a shock to the system at first, is to remove the time-zapping apps from your phone. This doesn't mean you don't engage in social media at all, but if it isn't on your phone, then it isn't with you every waking hour of every day. I made the conscious decision to remove certain apps from my phone and engage in social media only from my laptop or other device. If you remove the apps from your phone, you won't be tempted just because your phone is in your hand.

What this does is it stops you from mindlessly scrolling just to fill up time. When I now have a few minutes between meetings or find myself waiting in line for a sandwich, then I do other things with that time. Productive or happier things. That could be just talking to the person in line next to me, taking some deep breaths, or thinking about what my next priority is.

While it might feel difficult to delete apps off your phone initially, I've had clients say, "I thought it would be harder than it was. I can't believe how much calmer I now feel."

It's a conscious decision and one that can make a big difference if you want some time back in your week. I've had clients on group coaching calls say, "I just removed the app from my phone." They did it as we were talking about it. They'd often then say, "I feel sick just thinking about it!" Invariably, when we'd catch up the next week, they'd say something like, "I had no idea what a difference it would make! I had time to read a book. I stopped at the bus stop and just stared at the trees around me. I had thinking time."

It's a powerful feeling to get time back like that.

If you decide removing the relevant apps from your phone is too extreme and you want to keep your social media apps on your phone, another option is to turn your phone to black and white. If it's black and white, it doesn't look anywhere near as attractive. Photos don't look as engaging. However, you'll find it easier to stop scrolling. Chances are you'll find yourself saying, "Why am I looking at my phone? There's nothing pretty here."

When you see beautiful pictures, you get a dopamine hit. When you read your messages, dopamine hit. If you alter your activities so that you don't get that dopamine hit, then it just isn't the same experience. That's what turning your phone black and white is designed to do.

My clients who change their phone's setting to black and white typically tell me they reduce their phone time by about a third. Their phone is nowhere near as fun to look at anymore, but it frees them up to focus on other more important things in their lives.

The next option is easier to implement, but it's not as effective as the solutions above. Simply remove the apps that you spend the most time on from your home screen. Bury them in folders a few pages deep on your phone. When the apps are on your home page, it's too easy to just open them when you have a minute to spare and mindlessly scroll. The default is to click the home button and log on. If you need to perform a few swipes to find your preferred app, you're less likely to use it. This is because those few seconds swiping to locate the app give you a few seconds of pause, at least. You have a few seconds to consciously ask yourself, "Why am I using my phone? Is this how I want to spend my time right now?" If it is, then go for it. But you'll have the opportunity, at least, to back out if you want to. If you're waiting for a meeting to officially start, maybe chatting and connecting with the people who are also waiting is a much better use of your time.

One final suggestion builds on this option. Move the apps around on a regular basis, so that your brain doesn't get used to where they are on your phone. Kill the autopilot.

Social Media

1. Remove the culprits from your phone

2. Turn your phone to black and white

3. Turn off notifications

4. Move apps off your home screen

5. Move apps around each week

Which of these solutions could help you reduce your time spent on social media?

These are some practical ways to think through your relationship with your phone, particularly with your favorite social media apps. Create your own nudges to help you engage the way you want to engage and take back your time.

Notifications noise

When people assess their 168 hours each week, they often find another area where they can cut out time-wasters. Notifications.

One notification on your phone or laptop can quickly drag you into doing something that was not on your agenda. Performing an audit of the notifications settings on each of your devices is time well spent. When we hear a ping or see something flash to let us know we have a message, curiosity usually gets the better of us and we interrupt whatever we're doing to check the message. This often leads us down the path of unfocused and unnecessary activity.

Remember that study that showed that when you're in deep work and you're distracted for a couple of seconds, it takes about twenty-three minutes to get back to the same level of deep work that you were into? A three-second distraction isn't about losing those three seconds of time in your day. It's about breaking your concentration and flow, potentially leading you down a rabbit hole of less important work. If you're constantly pinged by people when you're trying to work, the ping wins. Simply remove the notifications where you can.

When you stop notifications, it's then up to you as to when you engage with the people wanting to contact you. You get to think, "I'm focused now, so I'll check my messages later when it suits me better." This puts you in the driver's seat. You're in control of your time and get to focus on your most important work.

Most of my clients are in large operational roles so they do need to be immediately available to address systems going down or other significant customer or employee issues. In these situations, it's about being clear which communications channels are for the highest severity issues and to keep notifications on either entirely for that channel or to keep them on only for certain people's notifications to get through, such as from your boss. The key is minimizing notifications in a way that enables you to still receive the urgent and important notifications while reducing the noise.

There was a study done by Rescue Time, which looked at the key reason people don't achieve their goals. The top reason given was distractions. Distractions are the number one thing that get in the way of you getting your best work done—the work that drives the most value for your people, your customers, and your organization. The more you minimize those distractions, the easier it is for you to focus on what matters most.

With my clients, we discuss and they agree as a leadership team which channels they will choose for communicating urgent issues. Notifications are kept on, sometimes only by sender, for those channels. Individuals then choose whether they turn off notifications for everything else.

Owning your calendar

For most corporate leaders, their calendar is the key tool that drives where they spend their work time. It therefore impacts their productivity and what they focus on significantly. As such, working through how to optimize this tool (or for your executive assistant to) is a great use of your time. A practical way to do this is to color-code your meetings in your calendar. If you accept every meeting invite you get and they are automatically added to your calendar, all your calendar entries end up looking the same. But not all meetings are as important as others. You need a way to prioritize them.

One practical way to do this is to color-code them based on level of importance. Which colors represent which level of importance is up to you. For me, I make all my big rocks (my most important meetings) one color. Those are things like delivering important presentations or meeting with top-level executives. Those meetings, I color-code green. Having all my most important meetings the same color means I can see at a quick glance when my big rock meetings are. The big rock meetings are non-movables. Once they're set, they are set and everything else is scheduled around them.

The next level of meetings on my calendar are important, but not as important as the big rock meetings. Examples include meetings about key strategic projects, meetings with mentors, or catch-up meetings with important stakeholders. I don't want to move those meetings if I don't have to, but I can if needed. I color-code them yellow.

The next category is important meetings or times when I'm unavailable outside of work. These are personal meetings like dropping the kids off at school, lunch dates, and my nonnegotiables, such as going for a run. All my personal meetings are purple.

As a rule, I block out noon to 1 p.m. Monday through Friday for lunch. If an important meeting pops up, that's OK. But to get that full hour so I can go for a walk, have lunch away from my desk, or some free personal time is important. Having it blocked out gives me my best chance at keeping it meeting-free. It helps make my afternoons more productive.

The last color in my diary is reserved for meetings that make sense for me to attend but aren't as important. I make those red.

When I look at my week, I can see my nonnegotiables at a glance. I can see all the important things going on in my life, how many big rocks I have, all my personal appointments, and anything already on the schedule. I can see where I can slip in some breaks and blocks for deep thinking or other productive work. I see whether I need to build preparation time into my calendar to be prepared for my big rock meetings. I see where my buffer times are for whatever issues might pop up unexpectedly.

Where practical, I then include two hours of buffer time each day. If nothing comes up that I need to use it for, then I look to see where makes the best sense to spend that time. Is there someone who needs a little extra coaching? Are there big projects or meetings coming up that I need to prepare for? What's next on my Ivy Lee task list to complete and cross off? This buffer time is color-coded red too, as it is movable.

Color coding your meetings doesn't take much time and can help you see what your priorities are at a glance, so you can ensure you make time for your urgent AND important work.

Multitasking is not efficient

When it comes to being efficient, multitasking is a fallacy. As mentioned, only 2 percent of the population have this ability. Therefore, for 98 percent of us, the best way to drive productivity is to focus on a single task at a time. When we think we're multitasking, e.g., answering an email while on a video call, we're actually dividing our attention. We're task switching.

Because we are switching tasks in our brain, we're not performing both at the same time. It happens in microseconds. It trains our brains to become distracted and it becomes harder to focus. We decrease our engagement in deep concentration, which is what we need for our best ideas to rise to the top, to make our best decisions, and our best work to come out. Studies show that we experience up to a 60 percent drop in productivity due to attempts at multitasking.[31]

This is very important to consider. When you are doing three things at once, you're progressing each task at different paces.

If you're on a video meeting and you find yourself checking your phone during the entire meeting, the question to ask yourself is, "Do I need to be in this meeting?" If you're not present and engaged, then it might not be the best use of your time. If it is, then put the phone away so you can focus on the meeting.

The Pomodoro technique

Another useful efficiency tool is called the Pomodoro technique and no, it's not about tomatoes. It's a time management tool that was introduced by Francesco Cirillo in the 1980s. Building on the concept of Parkinson's law and time-boxing tasks, you set your timer for twenty-five minutes and work on one task with all distractions (phone, notifications) minimized. Pairing this approach with your Ivy Lee task list really accelerates your impact. It's really that simple.

When the alarm goes off, take a five-minute break. It's based on the idea that productivity isn't about sitting at your desk for eight, ten, or twelve hours straight a day. Regular breaks are important to refresh your mind and body so you can be at your most effective. In other words, less is sometimes more.

You might end up doing fifty minutes of work and taking a ten-minute break if you can keep your concentration going that long. If you're new to the technique, you might work in shorter increments and take shorter breaks.

---

31 - *Ikagi: The Japanese Secret to a Long and Happy Life* by Hector Garcia and Francesc Miralles.

Maybe you work for fifteen minutes and take two-minute breaks. Whatever works for you. The important thing is to work on a single task for a concentrated period and then take a short break where you can clear your mind.

The Pomodoro technique also works for meetings. Simply schedule your meetings for twenty-five minutes so you can then take a five-minute break, or for fifty minutes followed by a ten-minute break. Many technology platforms now offer this functionality as something you can automatically build in. Meetings can default to twenty-five or fifty minutes when you schedule them. If your company doesn't use this feature, consider whether it's worth exploring.

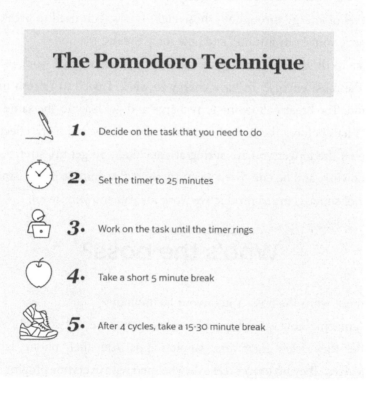

Time-boxing tasks helps you get through them more efficiently.

The time increments are flexible. My view is, if you're in the flow and close to finishing your task, it's fine to keep going for an extra ten minutes before you take a break.

When you're on a long road trip and you're driving, you don't drive for eight straight hours because you know your body will get tired. You know your mind will get tired and you need to recharge. You might drive for an hour or two, then stop and stretch, get some fresh air, and then go at it again. It's the same concept.

An eight-hour stint sitting in the same spot, doing the same activity, is going to lull you to fatigue. Your body will lag. You're not going to have the same level of energy throughout those eight hours. You need to break up the time, move your body around, and take some breaks.

I like to think about managing my energy levels when I work. When do I have the most energy? To have energy to work, I need to refresh my body and mind. The breaks allow me to recharge and get back to the same level of energy I had before. The data shows that productivity and work effectiveness slow down the longer you are sitting at your desk. So get up, stretch, get the blood flowing, and be energized again. A short five-minute break can unlock an hour of super-charged productive work for you and your team.

Who's the boss?

It's all about who's the boss. You or your technology?

It's amazing how quickly people realize they have lost control over their time after they delete their time-zapping apps from their phone, laptop, or other devices. They no longer feel overwhelmed with everyone pinging them at the same time. Constantly.

Ping. Ping. Ping.

Your colleagues, friends, and family may still be pinging you, but you get to choose when to become aware of this and engage. You're in control. You can check your messages when it's convenient for you. It not only frees up your time, but it also frees your mind too by easing the feeling of overwhelm. You can become more creative, innovative, and productive. The master of your own fate.

Focusing on your most important work—the work that drives the most value—is freeing. "Your inbox is someone else's to-do list," as my brother, Tim, would say.

This quote made me reflect on how I manage my emails and my inbox. About 80 percent of what typically came into my inbox was either information somebody else wanted me to know about in my own time, back-and-forth "reply all" emails that should have been a conversation, emails I was copied on (and probably shouldn't have been) or emails that could have been covered off as quick line items in one-on-one or team meetings. But it didn't necessarily mean that replying to all those emails or acting on them would drive real value for my people, my customers, or my organization.

This doesn't mean we shouldn't check or reply to our emails at all! In most corporate cultures, email is still one of the key tools used for requesting work to be done and communicating. The key is to proactively choose the windows that are the optimal time for you to manage your emails (e.g., 9 a.m., 1 p.m., 4 p.m. most days) so that you can be more effective in how you respond to emails and more effective as a leader overall. A *Harvard Business Review* study of twenty-seven CEOs of public companies worth an average of $US13.1 billion found that they spent on average 24 percent of their time on emails over the three-month time period.[32] By choosing specific times to check and respond to emails, you'll be able to spend less time checking email overall and more time focusing on your work that really matters. This can also "slow down" the back-and-forth emails that often occur—so that recipients can focus on what really matters.

---

32 - "An Analysis of CEOs' Schedules Scrutinised 60,000 hours and Found Email Is an Even Bigger Time Sink than People Realise," Myelle Lansat, 2018.

A few years ago, I was working in a senior role in a large global organization and was chatting with members of the technology team. One of the technology support gurus said to me, "Tina, do you know you've got a reputation for something?"

Intrigued, I asked, "What's that?"

He said, "You've got a reputation for not always answering your emails."

I burst out laughing. Then, with a big grin on my face, I said, "Spread it around!"

I loved that that's one of the things I was known for. I don't spend my day hiding behind my keyboard answering emails because I don't believe it's always the best use of my time as a leader. I'd rather be coaching others on a video call. I'd rather be at a whiteboard, whether virtually or in the office, dreaming up what's possible for the next three years. I'd rather be reflecting on how I can drive more value for my people, my customers, and my organization. I'd rather be focusing on doing or delegating the work to make it all happen.

If the cost of being an effective leader is having a reputation for not answering all my emails, then I am completely fine with that. To the core of my being, I believe the role of an effective leader is to drive value for your team, your customers, and your organization in a values-led way. It isn't to be the fastest person at responding to emails or to have an inbox with only two unread messages in it at any given time. That's not my measure of success. I don't know about you, but I've never seen response times to emails in a leader's annual goals or on their performance appraisal under the "achievements" section. I've never seen anyone promoted for this. If that's where your focus is and you have a desire to be known as the person who answers their email the fastest, then what is the cost of that reputation? What is the cost to your team? Your customers? Your organization?

I'm not saying don't read your emails or reply to any of them in a timely manner. Just consider where answering emails truly serves you well to do it as frequently as you are and to the same level of detail. Responding to specific emails can create those micro-moments of building and maintaining trust.

There are other options you can employ to reduce emails and still build those connections, though. My teams knew very clearly that answering emails wasn't my primary goal in my role.

Where practical, instead of my team each emailing me ten times a day, they would put each topic to discuss with me on a shared online list. We would then discuss all the non-time-sensitive items in our next one-on-one. Also, when I would start working with someone, whether it be a stakeholder or team member, I'd tell them up-front that my focus wasn't on my inbox and to text me regarding anything urgent. Once again, "clarity is kind." And if you're in an operational leadership role where turnaround time on customer, system, or employee issues is critical and you need to be immediately available, then consider which channels you'll use with your colleagues for urgent requests—and challenge if email is really optimal for urgent communications, particularly given the noise of all the other competing emails that come into your inbox.

Thinking about the barrage of emails I'd get most days reminds me of my first boss, Ian. It was February 1999, when company email was still relatively new and we didn't have smartphones. One day he said to me, "There will always be more work in your in-tray." In those days, we had in-trays and out-trays on our desks. Colleagues would put printed forms or requests for work to be done in our in-trays on our desks. We would then prioritize all those pieces of paper, work through them and put completed forms and other work in our out-trays on the other side of our computers. There were always more papers in that in-tray. In today's terms, this saying translates that it's typically an unrealistic expectation to constantly have an empty email inbox. There's usually a lot more work wanting your time and attention.

Unless you decide to make email management your full-time job (at the expense of other, more value-added work) or alternatively work one-hundred-hour weeks (usually at the expense of having other activities and people in your life), chances are you'll never get through everything. Focus on the important work that matters to your people, customers, and organization. Touch each email only once. Deal with it, delete it, or archive it in one storage folder so that it's easy to search for. And remember the important concept of your "to-don't" list.

Remember your SCD ratio? Implementing the practical strategies outlined here will free up a lot of your "doing" time, so you can focus your time and efforts on delivering extraordinary outcomes—without burnout.

CHAPTER 10

Remote Teams Can Change the World

Remote teams are here to stay. Leaders need to know that this is going to become our new normal.

One executive, Rob, shared a story with me to demonstrate how far we've come in the corporate world. Rob was the chair of a global committee that needed to have a two-hour meeting. The purpose of this meeting was to make a big decision, but one which was considered quite mechanical and the committee all knew each other relatively well. It was not a complex decision. Rob suggested that they meet virtually, all dialing in from their respective countries around the world. This suggestion was met with strong objection. *"The technology won't work!" "The time zones will make it hard!"* However, Rob pressed for this option, knowing it would save them all time and money commuting to one location. In the end, he had to compromise. The solution? The committee members flew into London, New York, or Hong Kong so they could stay in their respective time zones. They then dialed in from three screens—one in London, one in New York, and one in Hong Kong. We've come a long way since this type of thinking about how business should be done was prevalent.

Companies want to hire the best talent and many are realizing that their options are far greater if they can look outside expensive cities. There are fewer real estate costs associated with remote working. You can give employees auton-omy and more freedom, which is what they're asking for. And these benefits aren't at the expense of productivity.[33] There are many reasons why this way of working is not even the wave of the future. It's here now.

This book is like a butterfly that flaps its wings in some remote region lead-ing to a ripple that spreads around the world.

That's a big statement, but if you think about what comes with it, and implementing what you've read in this book, it will lead to you and your team having more freedom. It gives you the freedom to ask, "What else do I want from my life?" You can have a great job and a successful career. The fact that you can have this AND the things that are important to you outside of work is incredible.

Being able to have dinner with your family, to have time for physical fit-ness, to catch up with friends will increase your happiness and productivity. Having the time to take holidays and experience travel and adventure is possi-ble. A lot of other things are possible, too, when you implement the steps you find in this book.

Of course, it's not just about you. The impact doesn't stop there. It extends to your family. If you have children, you can raise them to see that you can have a career on your own terms. If that's what you choose, you can be a part of a large organization and do it your way.

You can role model for your children that you can have freedom and live life on your terms, even while working in a large organization. You can also create better outcomes for your customers. You can focus on the stuff that really matters. Your customers will win, your people will win, and your organization will win. And by delivering the right outcomes, you will also win.

As the world becomes increasingly more digital, it creates more connec-tions. One of the things that so many people talk about is a fear of losing out to technology. Technology can be brilliant. It can be used as a force for good or it

---

33 - *Remote Work Revolution* by Tsedal Neeley

can be a means of losing authentic connections with people. We must consider that connection and collaboration are important, not only in the workforce but also with our relationships outside of work.

Whether it be with your work colleagues or personal relationships outside of work, be sure to keep your connections and collaborations at the forefront of your mind. By unlearning some of the old ways of working that made you successful in the corporate world but no longer serve you, you can look after yourself and be happier, healthier, and even more productive. Throw off the long hours, get rid of exhaustion and overwhelm, and free yourself to focus on your "outcomes over hours in the office." Doing this will not only be time well spent, but can completely transform your life as well as for those around you.

It does not have to be hard

Greg McKeown has written two wonderful books titled *Essentialism* and *Effortless*. He asks a question in *Effortless*, which I love. He encourages readers to ask themselves, "What would this look like if it were easy?"

Often, I think we try to overcomplicate things. Easy doesn't mean lazy. As a leader, think through how to make your processes easy. Make it effortless to achieve great outcomes. It's a great use of your time to sit for an hour or two and think through how to make your job and that of your team easy. Cocreating a clear vision and strategy helps. As does building team connection and trust. As does recruiting and onboarding new hires well. As does creating a regular operating rhythm for team and individual check-ins. As does creating clear tracking, communication, and recognition of outcomes.

While writing this book, I had lunch with a friend who has also written a book. I asked her about her experience writing it. She said, "It was a labor of love. I put my heart, my blood, my sweat, and my tears into my book. I got up at 5 a.m. every morning for three and a half years to write it." She was so proud of it.

I said, "You have every right to be proud of the book you've written. It's outstanding."

But I took a different approach.

I thought through how to make writing this book easy. I wanted a similar outcome. I wanted to write a great book. I wanted it to be my best work possible, so I could share it with corporate leaders all around the world and help them with some of the lessons I've learned. But I wasn't going to get up at 5 a.m. for three and a half years to make it happen.

For me, thinking through what would make it easy involved dreaming up about how to engage other people to help me write the book. I had to have a conversation with my publisher. She interviewed me and helped me get all of my content, everything I've learned over the past twenty years, and all of the blood, sweat, and tears onto the pages. It was through conversation. As we recorded these interviews, we heard this click-clacking in the background as it was being automatically transcribed, so we had a shell to work with. You might have noticed that this book reads like I'm talking to you. That's because I am. In each interview, I have spoken as though I was chatting with you—an amazing leader working in corporate—and sharing what I've learned and now teach. That made it easy.

I share this because I think we sometimes take the hard road on things unnecessarily. But you don't have to do things the way they've always been done. Bridging this to office work, you don't have to be in the office eighty hours a week and be present when your boss is there, just because that's the way your boss did it. That's not easy. Think about what work would look like for you if it were easy.

When I asked myself this question as a corporate leader many years ago, I realized that the office wasn't the thing to focus on. My focus needed to be on the clarity of the vision, delivering on the outcomes that made the most difference, the connection and the trust, communication and collaboration between my team, our stakeholders and me.

That's when I realized that it's about the outcomes, not the hours in the office. We've got technology that can help us edit documents from anywhere at the same time. You can leave notes online for people to be super clear on what the work is, so you don't have to all be together in the same room. You can record online meetings for those who missed them to listen to later.

For me, making work easy meant that my team would have the freedom to bring their whole selves to work. They might need to leave work early to go to a school assembly and see their child receive an award or head out at lunch for a run, then come back to work a few hours later.

I encourage you to think through all the strategies I've put into this book for you. Use it as a blueprint and implement the parts that are relevant for you. What would your work look like if it were easy? How can you implement this plan with your team?

None of this is just theory. It all works. I've done it for over twenty years. The answer to the question "What would it look like if it were easy?" is to implement everything I've shared with you in this book. I've done the hard yards. I've spent thousands of hours working through what works and what doesn't so you don't have to.

Now, it's up to you to get out your highlighter and highlight the bits that will make the biggest impact for you and your team. Build the next generation of leaders who feel confident to lead and work from anywhere, so that you can leave a career legacy you'll be proud of and have the freedom to live life more on your own terms.

My clients tell me that working with me and implementing these strategies is life-changing for them. They feel more present with whoever they're with and that they can be themselves, whether at work or at home. They get their work done effectively and efficiently and have a wonderful feeling of accomplishment while progressing their careers. But they're also calmer, healthier, and more connected.

I love that feeling.

There's nothing more exciting for me than hearing from a client that the work we've done together has changed their life. But I want it to scale. I want that not only for the leadership teams I coach through my group coaching programs, but also for everyone who feels exhausted and overwhelmed by their work. For me, it's about getting this message and practical strategies to as many people around the world as I can, to help them achieve the life of their dreams. If I can do that, I'll feel like I've cracked the nut on something that a lot of other people have tried in different ways.

You can help me crack that nut by implementing these strategies in your own life, and let me know how it turns out.

Acknowledgments

First, I'd like to thank the team at Beverly Hills Publishing, particularly the amazing Andrea Albright. Andrea immediately got my vision for a future of work where people could have successful careers in large corporate organizations AND have the freedom and time to focus on what mattered most to them outside work, be it family, travel, sport, volunteering, or collecting miniature dolls. Thanks also to Allen Taylor, Cindi Hunnefeld, and Amanda Payne from Beverly Hills Publishing, who worked tirelessly to turn my words into the book that you're now reading. This book, and my business, simply wouldn't happen without my "A-team" of Shell Mirabella and Pip Crisp—talented and wonderful human beings who make work so meaningful and fun! And my clients, bosses, colleagues, and team members who have allowed me to share your stories—you know who you are and I thank you so much.

Second, to my amazing bosses and mentors in the corporate world, who have helped me evolve my thinking, practical strategies, and conviction that the future of work for corporates belongs to the companies that trust their leaders and teams to get the right work done, from wherever and whenever it suits. Special thanks go to Kaivan Desai, Christina Selby, Michael Ackland, David Moffatt, Ian Hamilton, Tanya Southey, Skander Malcolm, Matt Mansour, Paolo de Martin, Ketan Majmudar, Mike Abbott, Curtis Howse, Bob Binnie, Roberto Munoz, Ralph Falke, Eric Lim, Melanie Cook, Jacqui Walker, Dean Ireland, Joy Linton, Emily Amos, Naomi Attwood, Kate Dee, Kain Nunn, Dean Holden, Richard Bowden, Hisham El-Ansary, Evelyn Bourke, Dwayne Crombie, Lorna Stewart, Sami Yalavac, Andrew Peeler, Kathryn Porritt, Vaughan Paynter, and Conor O'Malley.

Third, to my teams who encouraged me to lead with the mantra "outcomes over hours in the office" and put their trust in me to lead in this way. There are so many of you who I learned from and so many of the strategies I share in this book come from our time together. You all know who you are and I hope you've had a smile on your face reliving our times working together, years before remote working became the new norm. Special thanks to Guneet, Sibu, Carlos, Shannon, Michael, Anna, Danielle, George, Cam, Narelle, Dean, Gem, and Megan—I'm so proud of where your careers have taken you.

Fourth, to my corporate network, many of whom came out of the woodwork to help me when they heard I was writing this book. To be able to say I've interviewed executives from companies such as Amazon, Microsoft, Cisco, GE, ServiceNow, Google, Accenture, KPMG, and Deloitte for this book is a real highlight for me. Thanks to Marty Drill, Naveen Menon, Connie Dudum, Ian Hamilton, Gabrielle Dolan, Ashley Haynes-Gaspar, Paul Davies, Mike Abbott, Sami Yalavac, Jo Thompson, Antonio Reza, James Cheo, Andrew Yates, Robert Hillard, Monique Landes, Susan Nicholson, Emma Doherty, Jen Rendell, Cassandra Goodman, and Carol Corzo.

Fifth, to my wonderful clients. Just as I was teaching you, I was also learning. Thanks for your authenticity and vulnerability at times to share with me your stories, so I could help you implement my strategies to get your work done effectively and look after yourselves and your teams. I'd particularly like to acknowledge my first ten clients, who were with me as I started with ugly PowerPoint presentations (I do look back on some of my hand-drawn models and cringe!). Special thanks to Tanya Southey, Megan Collins, Mel Bull, Shanyn Payne, Elizabeth Buchanan, Nat Peters, Mark Johnston, James Stewart, Adele Martin, Craig Redihough, Kerry Reid, Lisa Brookman, Hazel Thurlow, Kate Nelson, Ryan Biggs, Nidhi Bhatia, Emmanuelle Beccari, Rana Mukhaimer, Arika Ishio, Rachel Scheel, Ewa Priestley, Shlomit Gruman-Navot, Rafal Gembal, Simon Moorfield, Mithran Naiker, Beth Liley, Chris Jackson, Julia Edwards-Smith, and Andrew Bidese.

Sixth, many ideas I write about in this book are not new. I may have tweaked them, but I'm forever indebted to the following thought leaders: Tim Ferriss (your book *The 4-Hour Work Week* is my most gifted book to others—it lit the fire in me to see that I could take three-month sabbaticals every five years, I could work four day weeks in large jobs and I could create my life by design), Brené Brown, Stephen Covey, Simon Sinek, Adam Grant, Arianna Huffington, Aubrey Marcus, Amy Cuddy, Katy Milkman, James Clear, Greg McKeown, Chip & Dan Heath, Andy Frisella, Charles Duhigg, Gretchen Rubin, Bill Mitchell, Dominic Price, Tsedal Neeley, Jay Shetty, Robin Sharma, John McGrath, Mitch Albom, and Andrew Barnes.

And on a personal note, thanks to my family: to Mum for making sure I always knew what was really important in life and my brother, Tim, for consistently showing me what it looks like to live your life on your own terms. Even though not physically here anymore, I know my entrepreneurial dad would have loved the rebellious nature of this book shaking things up in the corporate world. To Judi, Jeff, Amy, Aart, Nic, Luke, Rose—you're all the family I would and do choose to have! And to my "circle of trust," my friends who've been there with me over the decades, SJ, Sam, Marth, Kish, Elise, Zo, Sar, Julia, Kath, Ing, Suz J., Suz G., Sus—you know what you all mean to me. ☺

And to my "three faves": my husband, James—there's no one I'd like to be sharing my life with more than you; our son, Angus—keep challenging the status quo as you do, as you truly can change the world (please just make sure you do it for the better!); and our daughter, Eliza—when people tell me I'm the most optimistic person they've met, I just smile and think of you—keep being that positive beacon making a difference in the lives of others. And finally, to my Gran Edna, who showed me that sometimes you've got to be the change you cannot yet see.

Made in the USA
Middletown, DE
01 April 2022

63470018R00106